THE SPIRIT OF ST. DOMINIC

THE SPIRIT OF ST. DOMINIC

Humbert Clerissac, O.P.

Edited and with a Preface by
Bernard Mulany, O.P.

With an Introduction by
Thomas Joseph White, O.P.

CLUNY
Providence, Rhode Island

Cluny Media edition, 2015

This Cluny edition includes minor editorial revisions to the original text
including deletion of obsolete references.

Additional translations by Meghan C. Lescault.

For more information regarding this title
or any other Cluny Media publication,
please write to info@clunymedia.com, or to
Cluny Media, P.O. Box 1664, Providence, RI, 02901

VISIT US AT WWW.CLUNYMEDIA.COM

ISBN: 978-1944418144

Nihil obstat:
Raymundus P. Devas, O.P.
Vincentius J. McNabb, O.P., S.T.M.

Imprimi potest: M.S. Gillet, O.P., S.T.P.

Imprimi potest: Reginaldus Phillips, S.Th.L, *censor deputatus*

Imprimatur: Leonellus Can. Evans, *Vicar General*
Westmonasterii, 14 November 1938

Cover design by Clarke & Clarke
Cover image: El Greco, *St. Dominic in Prayer*,
between 1600 and 1610, oil on canvas
Courtesy of Wikimedia Commons

To Jacques Maritain
to whose kindness and encouragement this
English edition of his friend's work is largely due

Vigilant enim et latrant boni canes et pro Domo
et pro Domino, et pro grege et pro pastore.

(Good watchdogs keep guard and give tongue for the
house and the master, for the flock and the shepherd.)

~St. Augustine

Contents

Preface

Father Humbert Clerissac was born at Roquemaure in France on October 15, 1864, and he died in 1914 just before the outbreak of the Great War. At the early age of sixteen his vocation dawned upon him after reading Père Lacordaire's *Life of Saint Dominic*; and during the thirty-four years of his Dominican life he showed forth a consuming ardour for the great ideal from which he never wavered. He was well known as a preacher in France, Italy, and England; and God manifestly blessed his ministry by many conversions. When the French anti-clerical laws scattered the Dominican and other communities in 1903, he went to London where he had hopes of making a French Dominican foundation. A variety of causes prevented the fulfilment of these hopes, and after a considerable stay in England, where he made many friends, he returned to France. His influence as a preacher and a director was very great indeed, especially upon the young men of the France immediately before the War, and he worked ceaselessly and indefatigably, giving retreats to religious men and women of his own and other Orders.

1

The absorbing enthusiasm of his life was for the ideals of his Father, St. Dominic. He would break out with an almost impatient zeal against those who were indifferent to so great a privilege as the Dominican vocation conferred upon them. Their obtuseness and unawareness would remind him of the words of Isaias who denounced "the dumb dogs not able to bark, seeing vain things, sleeping and loving dreams" (56:10). In a letter written just before he died he deplored the frightening possibility "of dying without having done anything for the Order. To bring others to understand and love its luminous spirit, the eternal youth of its doctrinal tradition, its exquisite large-mindedness, its sublime idealism—would not one willingly die to make that known and loved!"

The pages that follow surely prove that Père Clerissac did not die without having striven to fulfil his noble ambition.

The chapters that make up this book were originally retreat conferences preached in English by Père Clerissac to his Dominican brethren in England over twenty years ago. The work has been translated into French and Italian; but it has never before been published in English. An English edition under the title *Pro Domo et Domino*, prepared by the author in 1914, seems to have come to nothing because of his untimely and unexpected death towards the end of that year. The present edition is a revised version of the 1914 text, very kindly placed at my disposal by M. Jacques Maritain. Although Père Clerissac had a considerable command of the English language, he does not seem always to have been perfectly at his ease with the written word and he had not but it has been clearly necessary to revise very considerably with a view to the more exacting requirements of the printed word. Those who heard this Retreat preached at Hawkesyard in 1908 remember the Father's quaint apology at the end for his "bad language." In the spirit rather than the letter of that apology the text of this work has been revised and sometimes re-written. I have only attempted to make the lectures more readable, to diminish the foreign accent, and I hope in the process I have not altered the ideas or doctrine or spoiled the splendour of an attractive and inspiring personality which, I venture to think, shines through in spite of all encumbrances and obstacles.

– Fr. Bernard Mulany, O.P.

Introduction

Saint Dominic was born in Caleruega, Spain, in 1170. His mother, Blessed Jane of Aza, had a dream while she was pregnant with her son, in which she imagined him to be a dog kicking in her womb. She saw this dog running forth throughout Europe carrying a torch in its mouth, a prophetic image of the mendicant preacher who would run through the world to bring the light and fire of the Gospel to the hearts of his compatriots.

Humbert Clerissac was born in 1864 and died in 1914, 700 years after St. Dominic founded the Dominican Order. Much of his life as a Dominican was spent in itinerancy, in part due to the anti-religious legislation of the French secular government. His novitiate was in Switzerland and his priestly formation in Holland. After the dispersion of the Order by the Third Republic in 1903 he spent time in London, and frequently preached retreats in France and abroad.

This book is the fruit of one such retreat, preached in Hawesyard, England, in 1908 and edited by Fr. Bernard Mulany, O.P. It is a spiritual classic.

In these pages, Fr. Clerissac presents to us the essence of the Order of Preachers, giving an understanding of the heart of that religious order instituted by St. Dominic in 1216. How do the *Domini-canes*—"the dogs of God"—bear the torch of divine truth out into the world? *The Spirit of Saint Dominic* is a book of astonishing beauty due to its spiritual magnanimity, its theological precision, and its balance.

Aristotle defines magnanimity as greatness of soul, a virtue that avoids the extremes of both pride and pusillanimity. The magnanimous person strives to do great things while welcoming the qualities and contributions of others. St. Thomas Aquinas notes that Christian magnanimity is humble because it recognizes that all that is truly good in us comes from God, and that all great works of evangelical holiness stem from the grace of Christ. Fr. Clerissac's book is magnanimous because it seeks above all to promote holiness, to encourage others to strive to live in Christ in a way that is truly noble and truly humble. The Dominican Order exists first and foremost to be a school of sanctity and of the communication of holiness to others.

The analysis Fr. Clerissac gives is theologically precise. It is that of a theologian who writes with clarity and insight. What does the religious life of Dominican Order consist of? What are its ends and missions? How is the formation of the moral conscience to be understood? Why live a life of obedience? Here we see a mind trained in scholastic and metaphysical principles, one that is not dry or tepid but inspiring and luminous. This book seeks to discern through the many ages of the Dominican Order what its enduring essence consists of. Understanding comes to the assistance of love. If we grow in our knowledge of the genius of St. Dominic, we will grow in our capacity to love the evangelical work that he founded.

Finally, this is a work of balance. Fr. Clerissac sees that the Dominican Order is both "canonical" and apostolic. It is founded in a common life of study and prayer and it also tends outwardly to the evangelical apostolate. It is an Order with a doctrinal mission, concerned above all with the saving truth of divine revelation, but it is also an Order of divine love, that seeks to unite the hearts of human beings with the heart of Christ. The Order is entirely ecclesial, existing at the heart of the Church for the service of the Church; the Order is also integral, with its own unique traits and way of life that are a precious resource for the Church in every age.

A great work of spiritual theology has a perennial relevance. Such is the case with this book. What was said one hundred years ago applies also in the 21st century, in this 800th jubilee of the Dominican Order, and in each age of the Order. If we should wish to meditate upon the perennial grace given to the Order of Preachers, we should consider Fr. Clerissac's vision in *The Spirit of Saint Dominic*. His message is also our own, that of the "dogs of the Lord." May the fire of Christ's truth burn brightly in our world.

–Fr. Thomas Joseph White, O.P.

I

General Features of the Order

I should like in your company and with your help to make a progressive study of the Dominican idea. Let us begin by trying to look back and catch that general view of it which attracted us when we first felt the fascination of its appeal. It will be helpful to make our start by trying to recapture this point of view, superficial and external though it may appear. The general impression we get at first sight of some great building may be neither complete nor detailed, yet in most cases it is the truest representation of the original, as well as the most faithful and most striking image of what we have seen. We go back then and try to lay hold of that first enchantment which dawned upon us when the Order had for us all the freshness, wonder, and glory of a newly-discovered ideal.

The sympathetic observer of Dominican life and the careful student of our history will notice three main features standing out clearly.

The first of these is *complexity*.

Our friends praise the Order for its simplicity; and, in so doing, I think they are right. Still, it remains true that our life is highly complex and it is only after having had experience within the Order and having lived in faithful devotion to its ideals that we begin to discover the splendid unity and simplicity which bind together all the many elements of which it is composed.

By *complexity* we do not mean anything complicated, confused, or overelaborated. Complexity in our sense does not mean a multiplicity of fussy details any more than simplicity means a dull uniformity or an entire absence of interesting variety.

St. Dominic, luminous and glorious, shining with the reflected light of the morning of eternity when God generates His eternal Word—*ex utero ante luciferum genui te*—strikes us as a complex personality. It is far short of the truth to say that he was a marvelously balanced character; for balance in the moral order implies the poising of opposite forces and energies, equalizing them until they cancel out and render each other null. In St. Dominic equilibrium did not mean the neutralizing but the intensifying of the forces at work. His different qualities, controlled and brought under the sway of reason and grace, reached the absolute fullness of their natural and supernatural impetus. He was a man of study, of prayer and of action, and in each so excellent that whatever he does, he does it with the skill and sureness of a master. It is as if every one of his single qualities were his special outstanding virtue. His love of divine knowledge is of a unique freshness and fragrance. As a young man we find him a rare student—the type of the perfect undergraduate: he sells his books to succor the poor. In those days it was not a common thing for a university student to have books to sell, and it is perhaps not usual for students of our own time to sell their books, at least from the motive of charity. Later on in life he gathers his first little group of disciples around him at Toulouse and takes them with him to the famous Master Alexander Stavensby, the Englishman, to learn theology. During all the time of his apostolic activity, on all his journeys, he is never without his copy of St. Paul's Epistles. The most popular of his contributions to the life of the Church, the Rosary, is stamped with his virile intellectuality; because the Rosary, which has chiefly to do with reflection and contemplation, appeals first to man's mind: it is a method of prayer and also a method of preaching. And from the manner in which his successors in the office of Master of the Sacred Palace have understood and carried out their duties, we gather that he was called to that charge rather as a teacher than as a preacher. I insist on the intellectual character of St. Dominic's genius because, though all instinctively admit it, not all understand it. A complex personality made up of paradoxes and contrasts, St. Dominic is an intellectual, a student (one might almost say a don), yet he is also the Canon, dedicated to the solemn liturgical worship: and, added to all this, he is the preacher spending himself in a ceaseless round of apostolic work.

The life of the student—the intellectual life, as we call it— is by itself all-absorbing and exclusive. It will not even brook interference from the higher reaches of the soul—from the affective part, as we call it; and it cannot bear interruptions from the noisy world outside: it must not be distracted either from within or without. St. Dominic made of his soul an ordered unity. His intellectual life required for its completion the active work of the apostolate; and the deep and calm life of the heart was the very source from which he derived all the force and energy for his Christ-like work. Since St. Dominic's day the union of these two elements has been lamentably broken and one is sometimes sacrificed in the name of the other. St. Dominic may be taken as the living symbol of the aspirations of human nature: an intense intellectual curiosity, exalted and made glorious by faith;

a yearning for repose, for a kind of sabbath calm felt by the human heart; and the need for outlet, for expansion and action. These are the three spiritual dimensions: the life of the mind in study, the absorption in God by prayer and contemplation, and the outflow of the soul into apostolic action. These three are neither mutually exclusive nor contradictory: they are the height, breadth, and depth of the soul's life.

Hence we know what characteristics to look for in St. Dominic's Order. His true children will bear the family likeness. They will be contemplatives, teachers, and apostles. The temptation to family pride in such high-sounding titles will be checked by the burden and responsibility they place upon us. We are, by our laws, forbidden to suppress any of these elements or to allow any separation of one from the other as a deadly dismemberment. *Absit hoc aeternum!* Our saints are all crowned with this triple glory though each with individual and varying radiance; and in the conscience of every Dominican there exists, in spite of national differences, the same deep-rooted conviction that in order to be true to our vocation and to do our work as it should be done, we too must be stamped with this threefold characteristic of our holy Father. It is a touchstone of the real Dominican—a dictate of conscience, a test by which he can assess his worth as a child of St. Dominic.

The second notable feature of the Order is its *penitential character*. Dominican life bears the note of hardship and difficulty. Indeed, its very arduousness seems to have been deliberately aimed at by our first Fathers. These giants of the Middle Ages seem of set purpose to have gone out of their way to find outlet for the moral and physical energy in which they abounded. It almost frightens those who come into contact with it to contrast the very real austerities of the Order with its external charm and even brilliance. Still more striking is it to note the kind of obstinacy with which our Order has refused to give up or to mitigate the austerities that other Orders—even of the monastic type—have easily surrendered. Yet corporal austerities are the least of our hardships, and, with us, dispensation is not a mere merciful concession to weakness but a wise, all-embracing rule of life and a sane principle of mental and physical vigor.

A more real difficulty with us is the intellectual acceptance and assimilation of the very complexities of which I have spoken. The trials through which the Order has passed at various times have arisen precisely from the changing appreciation and temporary defeat of that complex and indivisible ideal. Remember the history of the chosen people whose story reads rather as if it were the history of monasticism in the Old Testament. Here is a people secluded from all other nations, especially called to an exclusively religious life, cut off from all profane pursuits, directly and immediately ruled by the divine will. The whole of its existence is to be explained by the struggle in it of a divine idea against the tendencies of the race. You know the vicissitudes in Israel of Monotheism and consequently of the messianic idea. The chosen people seems ever to be seeking escape either from the worship of the true God to idolatry, or from its mission as prophet and guardian of the messianic promise to alliance with strangers and compromise with God's enemies whom God had commanded not to be spared. The vocation of the Jewish people suggests points of resemblance with our own religious and apostolic life; and their history is, as it were, a shadow or type of the vicissitudes of our own history and of the struggle of one complex idea against the alternating ascendancy of one or other of its parts. We must admit and expect the initial difficulty of an exact understanding of our vocation. Later on I shall have many opportunities of pointing out to you the foes of our ideal; for the present it is enough to ask ourselves if we have the intellectual

courage to embrace in their fullness the fundamental principles
of the Order. Truly it is a sad thing to see a Dominican falling
short of his ideal, yet it is sadder still to see a Dominican who has
never grasped that ideal. To have eyes and yet not to see, marks
the spiritually blind; and such blindness is a more decisive proof
of lack of vocation than the lowest degree of unworthiness.

When Blessed Humbert says that St. Dominic took from
the Premonstratensian Constitutions whatever he found in them
that was difficult, beautiful, and wise—*quod arduum, quod decorum,
quod discretum*—he is referring to the practices of the regular
life, and in these words he pays tribute to the spirit of chivalry
of our early Fathers. Clearly they could not rest content with
what was easy or comfortable in any branch of life or any sphere
of action. In their delicate asceticism they deemed the beautiful
inseparable from the arduous and, let us add (for there was nothing of fanaticism in their penance), from wisdom too. Thus from
the very beginning there is a link, firm though not clamorously
asserted, between the spirit of St. Dominic and the spirit of St.
Paul—I mean a passionate longing for the wisdom of the Cross,
a heroic love for Jesus crucified. St. Dominic dreamt of shedding
his blood for the Gospel. His sons, as champions of the faith
and teachers of truth, had to face persecutions as bitter as those
endured by St. Paul. Our ensign, *Veritas*, is a challenge: it implies
a spirit of sacrifice and a thirst for conquest and yet a profound
calm and the imperturbability of a quiet heart.

Thirdly and finally, the Dominican Order seems to be
endowed with an especial charm and attraction. It is remarkable
to note in our primitive chronicles the number of times that
the word "gracious" is applied to certain qualities of speech
and ways of life which combine a joyous grace and easy elegance
with manly dignity and strength. *Gratiosus praedicator* is an oft-
repeated phrase; and it was for Dominicans that a Cistercian

monk of Siena wrote those prayers *pro Praedicatoribus* which
implore for us the *verbum gratiosum*. The early history of our
Order abounds in episodes in which the lives of our Brethren
appear in an attractive splendor—ingenuous sometimes and of
an exquisite simplicity which it is almost a profanation to quote
in the hearing of modern ears. We know of St. Dominic's many
friendships and of his natural genius, which grace elevated for
the cause of winning souls to God. This spirit of St. Dominic has
drawn many souls to the Order.

The attraction and charm of the Order come upon religious
minds in many different ways. For some the life of the Church
is envisaged as a mighty hunt for souls. God is the hunter, the
apostles the huntsmen; the prayers of the saints thrill through
the air like a noble hunting song; on all sides are seen rebel and
timid souls fleeing from the approach of divine grace; the pack
breaks forth and the cry goes up as they give tongue. Who would
not wish to join the hounds of St. Dominic? Again, to other
souls the Order appears as a vision of the stately portals that
open into a kingdom of divine knowledge; and an unending
vista through fields of ever-growing light invites the mind athirst
for the heavenly realities. Love and understanding, innocence
and repentance, action and contemplation all bloom and fruc-
tify in the garden of St. Dominic. How are we to explain this
appeal of the Order? It is easier to recognize it than to analyze
and define it. It is in some way explained if we remember that
the Order came into being just when an age of spontaneity was
coming to an end. The analyzing temper tends to mutilate the
living essence to which it applies itself. The introspective spirit
is like a kind of soul-tinkering which tampers with the mainsprings of life. "He who gives ear to his own speech listens to
a fool": in the same way he who dissects his own life dissects
what is not far removed from the condition of a corpse. But in

its golden age the Dominican Order appeals to us as something unselfconscious, natural, spontaneous, and gloriously alive. If we did not know what very manly men those early friars were, if our Constitutions did not remind us of how very hard they were on themselves, we might be misled sometimes into thinking they had the minds of children, that their self-distrust was a kind of pusillanimity or that the delicacy and tenderness of their devotion had somehow enfeebled them and rendered them soft and credulous. In this way they are depicted by those historians who write fantasies about the Middle Ages and refute themselves in the same breath by the terrible pictures they draw of the bloodthirsty inquisitors. The truth is that our Order was, with that of St. Francis, though in a different way, the last efflorescence of the childlike spirit of the Middle Ages.

But the whole point of the Order's charm is to be found in the fact that it has something else along with its ingenuousness: it has a gigantic intellectual mission. That frank simplicity which charms us in a child is only tolerable when allied or contrasted with other gifts; and the ingenuous spirit is only charming even in a child when it goes along with intelligence. We are bound to admit that we Dominicans have displayed in the various spheres of our activity not only the virtues but also the defects that spring from this contrast—for instance, we have sometimes shown a perilous aloofness and disinterestedness, an irrepressible sincerity, an almost tactless disregard of persons, and a genius for being unpractical which would have ruined any other institution. We have heard it stressed too much perhaps that we are adventurers —on an adventure of truth. It would be a pity to overdo this and make out the Order as something excessively romantic.

The charm that belongs to the Order is the charm that belongs to ancient nobility—something massive, even rugged and unpolished, but genuine, solid, and true: it is that gracious quality that springs from wisdom, and knowledge and is moved by a passionate love of our human kind. Victor Hugo idealizes Torquemada in an ingenious way and shows him extinguishing the fires of hell and lighting the fires of the Inquisition. No such forced effort is needed when we are thinking of St. Dominic. His gracious influence works by its own force; and no legendary calumny can impair it. It penetrates into the depths of men's souls with a grace and power which are so gentle and mysterious as to be indefinable and almost imperceptible; and though of a severe purity, this charm includes all the different forms of attraction in which we have seen the vision of the Order manifesting itself to souls. The rays that shine from the star on St. Dominic's forehead are as varied as they are glorious.

We must remember that we are the custodians of the spirit of St. Dominic—the guardians in a sense of that charm which enthralled our souls on the day when our vocation dawned. We must keep that treasure in face of the withering blast of skepticism and from all other base alloy. We have in our own way to reflect that spirit as St. Dominic himself caught its reflection from Our Lord. We must not lose sight of St. Dominic's star: we must help others to grasp more fully its meaning and to embrace with brave hearts the complexity and difficulty of the Dominican ideal—as it is said of our saints in the Breviary: *ita ut partes omnes Instituti quod amplexus fuerat, cumulatissime expleret.*

II

The Apostolate

Our Order was founded for the salvation of souls: the apostolate is its aim and end. It is needless to quote the text from the Constitutions which assert it, but I wonder whether we ourselves always fully grasp the true notion of the Dominican apostolate. Let us try to see first the Church's original idea of St. Dominic's mission; secondly, whether a reawakening of that apostolic idea is not urgently needed among us today.

In such matters everything depends on the intention of the Church. I do not mean that the Church creates founders and saints, according to her good pleasure, "but no man taketh honor unto himself without both vocation from God and mandate from the Church." In the famous Bull of Honorius III, given from St. Sabina on December 22, 1216, to St. Dominic, the Pope calls the first Dominicans "champions of the Faith and true lights of the world." These words echo those of Our Lord, "Let your loins be girt and lamps burning in your hands," and again, "You are the light of the world." By connecting the Church's words with those of Our Lord we see that the prophetic praise of the Pope was no excessive metaphor. Indeed, the apostolic mission of the Order can be traced back to the very idea of the apostolate of the early Church. We need not delay to admire the statuesque beauty of this image, which represents so vividly the part the apostle plays, both as defender and enlightener: we will only seek to elicit from the words the two characteristics of the ministry entrusted to St. Dominic and to his sons.

The first characteristic is that a champion is more than a mere soldier; a champion is one who in some special crisis officially and solemnly represents a great cause or a great country: the mere soldier represents it but vaguely. A champion of truth is no mere instrument of defense, but is identified with the truth; he himself, the living personification of justice and truth, is as much to be dreaded as his blows. He comes to avenge a cause, and the issue of the single combat is definite and final: his mission carries with it the weight of a kind of judicial power; his rights are more than any personal rights, they are the rights of the cause he represents. Only so vested can the fighting man claim to be a champion.

The distinguishing marks of the Dominican apostolate from the beginning have been its championing of the truth and its participation in the doctrinal and judicial power of the Church.

Preaching is the official function of the Bishops as successors of the Apostles, and of right, belongs to them alone. Before St. Dominic's time, priests "were, under special circumstances, delegated to preach, but only in a restricted sphere. St. Dominic raised the preacher to a certain official participation in the doctrinal mission of the Bishops. Thanks to him, the preacher can lay a certain claim to the title of doctor; and to St. Dominic, not only we his sons, but also all priests owe a more extensive appreciation and exercise of their mission. This was a revival of the true conception of the priestly function in the Church, a revival which links the individual action of the priest with the mission of the Apostles themselves.

This sharing in the apostolic and doctrinal power of the Bishops has been reinforced and increased among us by a very clear and definite participation in the Church's judicial power as well. St. Dominic appears, in his campaign against the Albigenses, as it were, an Inquisitor in anticipation; and soon afterwards the Church specially entrusted us with that office, which the world, for good or evil, has ever associated with the Dominican name. Thus in St. Dominic the idea of championship finds its full development, and his Order is identified with the cause and the honor of Truth.

The other characteristic to be derived from the words of Honorius III is the universality of the apostolate as renewed by St. Dominic. The manner in which he acted towards the Holy See, though marked by singular courage and daring, was so tempered by an unobtrusive modesty that it blinds us to the greatness of his undertaking. I do not hesitate to say that, since the days of St. Paul, no venture of such great weight and importance had even been attempted. St. Paul's special work had been the universalizing of the Gospel in the sense of liberating the action of grace from the bondage of the law and delivering it as the common heritage of all—Gentile, Jew, and the whole human race. This is, as you know, the fundamental idea of the Epistle to the Romans and the motto of St. Paul might well have been "*Gratia Dei non est alligata.*" St. Dominic's apostolic action was much the same, or perhaps I ought to say that in this he is only following out the apostolate of St. Paul from whom he might have borrowed the motto, "*Verbum Dei non est alligatum.*" It seems to me that, in his idea and in his mission, he is even greater than any of those apostolic men who, at various times and in barbaric ages, have been sent to convert a nation. His mission, and that of his Order after him, was to the entire world. No doubt for him the Cumans represented the uttermost bounds of the earth. In any case the idea that God confides to a man is of greater importance than any personal action of his can ever be. St. Dominic was the herald who recalled to the mind of the Church the words of the Master, "Go, teach all nations." And the Church recognized this personification of the Catholic apostolate in St. Dominic when Pope Honorius III placed under this new founder's authority even preachers belonging to the older monastic Orders in view of a general campaign in Italy (Letter of Honorius III, May 12, 1220.)

Reflect how difficult it is for us to step outside the little groove of our individual lives. It would be a strange enigma, were it not so easy to understand, that men should have so great a shrinking from what develops and ennobles them. A man needs exceptional powers to be able to feel with certitude that he has the right to overstep the little boundaries of his ordinary sphere of action, and to feel sure that he is rich enough in gifts of thought and heart to distribute them among the nations of the earth. St. Dominic's conception of the apostolate was limited neither as to place nor method. By his intuitive and, I might also say, instinctive realization of this great idea he manifests a thirst for souls at least as great as that which finds expression in the burning words of the apostles of other ages. St. Dominic's cry to God seems not merely to have been: "Let me give Thee the souls of this people," but "Let me give Thee the souls of all the world." "Having been defeated in Languedoc, hero that he was, he determined to conquer the world. Savior that he was, he saw that the wound to be healed was not of a province, but worldwide and world-deep" (Fr. Vincent McNabb.) To sum up: the two characteristics that mark St. Dominic's apostolate concern its quality and extension. Thanks to him, the apostolate has again become what it was to St. Paul: dogma quickened to life and action; divine truth, loved

and taught for its own sake; contemplation and mystical life overflowing into wondrous activity; supernatural revelation ordering
towards its end all branches of natural knowledge; the unity and
happiness of mankind bound up with the unity of the Church.
By its universality the Dominican apostolate becomes a mighty
instrument of action in the hands of the Catholic Church. Alter-
natively, it is a trumpet and a sword, but in the thought of St.
Dominic, the hand that moves it is ever that of Rome. We may
regret that we have not received more frequently in these days the
direct impulse of that central authority. In any case, the placing
of such an instrument at the disposal of the Church is equivalent
to a vow of loyalty to the Holy See.

Originality in a man means either the invention of something new, or the combination in a new way of things already
existing. We have seen that St. Dominic united three different
elements in a new form of life; he also invented something new,
or rather, what comes to the same thing, he restored and put in
a new light the doctrinal and universal character of the apostolate. It is most fitting that he should have received from the holy
Apostles, Peter and Paul, the staff and the book. What wonder
that we find him, when he sends forth his disciples, using Our
Lord's own words, "Going therefore into the whole world preach
the Gospel to every creature."

Is there any need to question the necessity of a reawakening
of the apostolate as conceived by St. Dominic?

If we remember that the apostolate is both a force and a
method, a genius and a science, a burning flame and a strategy, we
shall of necessity recognize that this antinomy presents a difficult
problem. When an earnest priest or religious has for years worked
on classic lines, inevitably he will call to mind the words of Our
Lord: "I am come to cast fire on the earth," and he will long to do
his share in enkindling that fire. After many a sermon and much

weariness, he will recognize that he is an unprofitable servant; but he may well ask himself whether this unworthiness is not largely due to the fact that he has not thrown himself heart and soul (and perhaps even outside the beaten track) into the work for the conquest of souls. Doubtless obedience will reassure him here; it is obedience which measures for him the task and even the harvest; but, while submitting, he is led to desire that obedience should demand more from him: he remembers that God, in the course of the Church's history, renews His laborers from time to time, to give new zest to the apostolate. He is tempted to think that he excuses the coldness of his zeal by solutions of casuistry and he cannot but fear in spite of all lest God should ask from him a terrible account for having restrained the force and obscured the flame, giving too great a share to the method and the system. Yes, with due respect to authority, we can ask such questions as these. The proof is that, in our own history, generally speaking, the initiative of individuals has created more than the impetus and inaugurating from official sources. At least we may desire and pray that the apostolate of the Order may clothe itself with the fullness of the character that St. Dominic intended it to have.

Let us face three very serious facts with which our apostolate has to reckon: the knowledge of these three will act as a spur to our zeal, will curb only our false discretion, and inflame our hearts with zeal worthy of the name.

The first fact, which is a tremendous feature of the modern age, is the dedication of the word to secular and profane uses. Nowadays everybody speaks, lectures, teaches, and even preaches. The question: "How shall a man preach, unless he be sent?" is quite out of date. Even in the Church there are many ways of eluding the import of our mission. The result is the weakening and enervating of the word of God. How isolated we feel among that crowd of self-appointed preachers; how feebly echoes the true Gospel message in that tumult of voices! Still more, we feel that we are besieged and pillaged; our message is torn from us, bit by bit, to adapt it to all kinds of human and fantastic views which alter its meaning. Criticism and journalism can no longer avoid giving to their readers, day by day, a hash of religious philosophy. We are strangers to the teaching life of the Universities, where of old we were citizens. I will not speak of the powerful influences, even in questions of religious and scientific knowledge, vested in the hands of politicians. Those whose province it is to be taught go to other masters than to us, and soon we will have no other hearers than a handful of well-meaning and harmless folk. Our deadly danger under such conditions would be to let our message be utterly torn from us, or, worse still, to attempt to adulterate or weaken it under the pretext of getting it more easily accepted.

Such lack of faith and courage may take a still lower form: when within the Church we see so many new foundations arise for the conquest of souls, we might feel disposed either to look upon them as contemptible rivals from whom there is nothing to learn, or as competitors who have already beaten us and in whose favor we must gracefully stand aside and, as it were, abdicate. The double shame would be both to abdicate and to speak evil, and truly we are apt enough to do both. This is a sad illusion. We need be envious of none: there is always room for us in the world, if we only jealously preserve our means of action, which the methods of others will never supplant. At the same time, this conviction should not make us so proud that we refuse to profit by the lessons of zeal and courage afforded by those younger than ourselves. The complexity of our life should not be for us an impediment but, on the contrary, an accumulative power of ever-fresh activity. I loathe to hear some among us continually criticizing the faults of others, instead of imitating what is good in them. No abdication, no adulteration, no envy! Let us remember the confidence of our Father, St. Dominic, in the power and strength of the Divine Word. His mission against the Albigenses had not been a complete success; other men would probably have been discouraged and would have given in. The true apostle, should he be occasionally obliged to cast the dust off his feet on a city or a town, will never cast the dust off his feet on the whole world. St. Dominic curses the Albigenses (in terms which remind us of Our Lord Himself), but he scatters his seventeen disciples and sends them to convert the world. And so St. Dominic, having labored with incomplete success, in that very hour dreamt of establishing a universal Order of Preachers. Divine as it is, the word of salvation in great measure depends for its results on our faith in it. It struck me like a blasphemy against the Order when I once heard an old Dominican say that our Order has had its day and that it must now be content to remain just a specimen of the past, without any promise or hope for the future. If this were true, we might as well exhibit the Dominican habit in a museum and place our Constitutions among the curios in a public library.

There is a second fact still more remarkable than the first, I will not call it the conflict of the great modern tendencies— scientific, social, and mystic— with Christian Revelation, but rather their convergence on the religious unity of mankind, whatever that may be in the minds of their leaders. No doubt in every age there has been the scientific question, not always as is the case today implying philosophical riddles, historical problems, and exegesis. Under the varying forms of serfdom and pauperism the social question has always been with us. Between the extreme forms of illuminism and quietism, mysticism has found its expression in many different forms. But in the present day these tendencies present special features which give them new life. Each of these three tendencies borrows from the other and gives back something of its own life in return: science pretends to be a religion; socialism claims to be a code of ethics and manifests a feverish worship of justice; mysticism in its turn asserts its right to be scientific. Moreover, these three tendencies concur and unite in holding out a definite promise either of an experimental knowledge of God or the deification of man. I do not think that it is an exaggerated view to see in this the greatest event in history since the barbarian invasions. We should look at it as something very different from a mere manifestation of blind forces. We should be awake to the seductive power of those tendencies which on every side are captivating intellects and souls, and we should be alive to the gravity and inevitableness of the transformation they bring about. A frequent fault with Catholics, as history plainly shows, is want of foresight, and an almost childish attitude in face of any grave crisis. We might almost say that this was the reason why Our Lord so insistently predicted the destruction of Jerusalem and the end of the world. We may find a deep lesson in the expectation of the coming of Our Lord which was so marked a feature of the Apostolic Age. As a consequence of our imprudent attitude, we have been without means of defense, devoid of all organization, and cowardly in the hour of danger.

Now I dare to say that there are three special reasons for us to review frankly the exceptional situation which lies at our door and to excite our apostolic zeal in the measure of its gravity.

First, in the very action of these tendencies a sacred cause is involved; I mean not only the interests of souls, but also the fact that these tendencies are fraught with supreme interest for the Church herself. If we duly gauge them, we shall see that they bear in themselves vast possibilities for her future, since they contain the germs of the unification of the religious thought of mankind in the body of Catholic doctrine. Is there a single Dominican who would not feel his heart throb at the thought of such a prospect? Is there any Dominican who would not long to work for its realization?

Secondly, our Order in its Golden Age gave an example of a generous understanding of the universal needs of its times. There is under the generalship of Blessed John the Teutonic a fact which deserves serious consideration and has special weight in our own day, I mean our quasi-status of wandering friars whose official records (still extant), dated from Asia and Africa, ring with heroic courage, and with almost too sanguine hopes for the conversion of the world. Remember what St. Catherine said in her Dialogue of our first Fathers: "Each seemed to be another St. Paul." When a certain Chapter appealed to their zeal, they all came forward as one man, begging to be sent. We seem to hear in our primitive history the echo of the words of St. Paul: ""Woe to me if I preach not the Gospel."

In the third place, is there not a call and a sign of Divine Providence in the fact that, in spite of our small numbers, we have had, and still have, the men to deal with the requirements of the present age? Specialists in History, Assyriology, Exegesis, and even in Sociology have sprung up among us in unexpected circumstances in which the hand of God is plainly seen. Though we have many opponents, though rare opportunities were missed by us under the Pontificate of Leo XIII, yet it is clear that much is still expected from us. Friends and foes alike feel that it is easier to forgive us for evil than to pardon in us mediocrity. Let us believe that the genius of our Order meets in a very direct way the needs of minds and hearts, not of this age only, but of all ages, since the freshness and youth of *Veritas* are eternal. We should remember what St. Ambrose says of the duty of intellectual charity: "*Similiter ut dives qui pecuniam suam non impartit pauperibus, ita etiam qui doctrinae suae gratiam non dividit imperitis, docere cum possit, haud mediocris reus est culpae.*" (In Luc. viii.) "Just as a rich man who withholds his wealth from the poor, so is he blameworthy who, when he could teach, neglects to share the riches of his wisdom with the unlearned."

There is a third fact to be considered regarding the question of the reawakening of our apostolate. In some countries the Order has, on account of special circumstances, been obliged to take charge of parishes or missions. Do not imagine for a moment that I wish to blame this adaptation to local needs, or that I shut my eyes to the fact that in France our restoration may come in this way. But I deprecate it in so far as it may be taken to imply a definite sacrifice of any of the three essential elements of our life: study, canonical life, and universal apostolate. The interests of the parish itself demand the preservation of our Dominican life in its integrity, for if that life of ours is not rich enough to overflow into that of those entrusted to us, then the level of the parochial life itself will be lower than that of any secular parish. Hence if, at times, it behooves the Order to make the sacrifice of devoting a certain number of its subjects to parochial work, then in return the parish must be as far as possible incorporated in and assimilated to the perfect life of the community. The parish must, to a certain extent, participate in the liturgical and intellectual life of the Fathers by breathing the atmosphere and assimilating the spirit of the Order: it must be initiated into a higher degree of the spiritual life. It must imbibe a spirit of devotion, marked with the special features of our asceticism, and ultimately be led to the imitation of our Saints, both of their interior life and of their labors for the Church.

Considered in this light, the parish becomes a field of special and intense culture, not to say a powerhouse, while the Order in its turn retains its power of extension. Both these results are lost if any of the essential elements of our life are sacrificed to the rush of parochial work.

In conclusion, it is not rash to wish for a renewal of the Dominican apostolate, and even to acknowledge, while we beat our breasts, that we have lost something of the necessary faith in the power of the Divine Word, and allowed to grow dim in our hands the torch of St. Dominic. In magnificent verse, Dante strongly reminds us of the dauntless impetus and of the worldwide results of the Dominican apostolate, first in our holy Patriarch and then in his sons:

> Then, with sage doctrine and good will to help,
> Forth on his great apostleship he fared,
> Like torrent bursting from a lofty vein;
> And dashing 'gainst the stocks of heresy,
> Smote fiercest, where resistance was most stout.
> Thence many rivulets have since been turned,
> Over the garden Catholic to lead
> Their living waters, and have fed its plants.
>
> (*Paradiso*, XII:97–106.)

III

The Exercise
of the Apostolic Office

After having considered the general characteristics of our Order, and admitted the necessity of a rekindling of the apostolic flame, let us come to the consideration of the exercise of this office. I propose to treat this subject in such a way that what I say may apply even to secular Tertiaries living in the world. It is therefore all the more clear that there is nothing out of place in speaking of it to those who are fitting themselves to be apostles. Those who are qualifying for the apostolate need a long preparation as well as the continual help of the prayers and merits of the faithful.

Three things present themselves for examination: the apostolic attitude of mind, apostolic conduct, and the apostolic ministry itself.

It is said of the *end* in the abstract, that it is *primum in intentione, ultimum in executione*; the first thing to be aimed at, the last to be achieved. Let us take this statement as a directive and moral principle. I mean that the apostolic end ought not only to rule our thoughts by right, but also to command them in fact. Since this is the end of our vocation, it must take the first place in our thoughts of the future; it must be our most ardent and supreme desire, and become an intention so carefully cherished that it is already invested in anticipation with a share in the efficacious power of our future work. We know that Our Lord desired to accomplish our redemption long before He was nailed to the Cross, and even long before He began in His sacred humanity "to do and to teach"; and you know in what terms He speaks of that desire. It is for Him a baptism of blood with which He had to be baptized: that thought was, as He said at the well of Samaria, His daily food. With us, too, our apostolic work should have its beginning in the depths of our hearts: the predominance in us of the apostolic intention is our first conformity to the mind and soul of Our Lord.

You will not be tempted to give to that intention the character of a vain and empty dream, or of a mere human ambition, if you take heed to maintain in it the double character of the Dominican apostolate. Hence you must not take low or unworthy views of your apostolic career. Beware of any thoughts of self-interest, or self-glorification. Remember you have before you, all in one, a doctrinal mission, a chivalrous duty, and a judicial office. Besides, it is certain that the more you give to your apostolic ambitions the note of universality, the less will they be in danger of self-interest. Thus the true sign that you enter into the apostolic attitude of mind will be if this intention renders you more fervent, and excites in you a greater thirst for true knowledge of divine science. It is often said that you people of England, like the ancient Romans, are destined not only to establish a vast empire, but also thereby to promote the moral unity of nations. It is impossible to conceive a true son of St. Dominic devoid of an ambition equally great. This is one of the many points of contact that some people love to point out between your national character and that of the Order.

In the person of St. Dominic, the apostolic intention appears clothed with an infinite tenderness. You remember how, seeing a city afar off, he wept over it, and the Breviary gives us the very words of the first chroniclers, when it says: *Peccatis et aerumnis humanis vehementer discruciabatur.* He was grievously afflicted by the sins and miseries of mankind. In a mere man, universality of affection excludes, as a general rule, such a degree of tenderness, but in St. Dominic the union of these two elements is a proof of his likeness to Our Lord, so that St. Catherine even dared to compare him with the Incarnate Word.

For you, part of the merit of your passion for souls consists in the long expectation and patience involved in your condition as students. You must contemplate it from afar, since in a sense, literally true for you, the end is the last thing to be achieved, *ultimum in executione* (so I will not incur the reproach of prematurely stirring your imagination and agitating your souls). Moreover, your apostolic desires may in the meantime be tried by all sorts of disappointments and contradictions. Obedience itself may some day apparently check them, but nothing, save your own unworthiness, can crush in your souls that great motive-power from which all your apostolic activity must proceed. Of us all, it is true to say that the end is the last in execution. The more we work, the more we feel that we fall short of the ideal of the Dominican apostolate. So that finally we regret the happy days of remote preparation, when the simple desire of our young hearts bore such great possibilities before God. Therefore do not think the preparation too long, and remember that Our Lord prepared Himself for thirty years for His active ministry.

All that we have to say of conduct may be summed up in a rule which—as we know from the answers of three witnesses to the Commissioners of Gregory IX—St. Dominic laid down in the primitive Constitutions; in this, his sons are commanded to speak only "to God and of God." Such a rule is indeed a hard saying to worldly frivolity and human respect. There is but one great saint, who could have made it obligatory in an Order destined to continual contact with men. How I wish we would oftener take it as a subject of meditation and self-examination. It determines the direction of all our interior activity, since speaking with God and having continual and intimate converse with Him, is that which on earth is most akin to the life in Heaven. Here once more, St. Dominic joins hands with St. Paul, who states as a matter of course that our conversation is in Heaven. To speak with God is the sum total of proximate preparation for the apostolate, for how could you speak of God if you are not already on speaking terms with God? All the long process of the art of prayer, the necessary detachment, mortification, and perseverance, tends only to that. It is necessary, when we speak to the world, that the world should recognize that we have just left the divine Presence. Surely on this there is no need to insist further.

I would almost say that the art of speaking of God is nearly as rare as the grace of speaking to Him. For, note well, St. Dominic here alludes rather to private conversation than to speech from the pulpit; he wishes one and the other to be full of God, and let us not hesitate to emphasize his words—*of God alone.* It is obvious that this rule is not meant to make us dull, indiscreet, or disagreeable: it must be explained exactly in the same way as the Gospel precept of unceasing prayer. But the most elementary meaning we can attribute to these words is that our private and habitual conversation ought not to be out of harmony with our public teaching and preaching. Nothing is sadder than to see the preacher, when out of the pulpit, by his life giving the lie to all the great truths he has taught or even failing to show forth the supernatural effect of the convictions he has expressed. That rule of speaking of God would, if well observed, oblige us, as a condition and a consequence, not to do anything that might contradict our words: it is therefore an adequate rule of conduct. Now we transgress it when we lack courage to talk of God. How often in a conversation that meandered through nonsensical nothings were we expected to say the word which would have struck the keynote of the lost chord of truth—and we had nothing to say! I do not speak of graver cases in which our silence may even have involved treason to truth and virtue. It is deplorable when a priest is flattered by a reputation for being a man of the world, which generally means that he would feel embarrassed to be taken for a man of God. I cannot count the numberless instances I have myself known of the severity with which such worldliness and snobbery were soon afterwards judged. May I here quote the only qualification that a certain religious brought back from a mission in which he thought he had been a success. "Father X is a very good companion and jolly good fellow,"† was the comment written to his Prior. There is but one way in which a priest can truly show good breeding, and it is in being essentially a man of God; and we must be blind indeed if we do not see the excellence and beauty of this real mark of noble birth.

It seems to me that in this country there are two opposite extremes, men either talk too much of God or too little. I am afraid that priests and religious err in the latter way. Of course, at times it needs an effort to bring to bear on social life the sacred functions with which we are invested. There may even be in that hesitation a very natural sensitiveness; yet, while many who are neither priests nor apostles attempt in every place and time to play a sacred part and strike a religious note, he who really bears in himself the sacred character ought not to forget that he is the salt of the earth. Surely, a candid outburst, and even an occasional explosion of faith and zeal, are preferable to a continual and

---

† In French, "Un bon commensal."

systematic reticence. The one thing necessary is that the world should echo the divine accent. It is said of St. Stephen, "Those who disputed with him were unable to resist the wisdom and the spirit of God which spoke through him." (Acts 6:10.) Again: "The judges looking at him, saw his face as it were the face of an angel" (Acts 6:15)—and thus should it be said of every one of us.

As to the ministry itself—I cannot attempt here to give you a treatise on our apostolic ministry. I do, however, wish first to emphasize its utter and absolute importance by bringing into prominence the likeness between those who have the care of souls and those who have the care of the bodily health of men. All that we can say of our relations with souls is expressed in this one word: our action is one of life and death. I am more and more impressed by the analogy between the treatment of the body and of the soul, between the priest and the doctor. He who preaches to a great congregation is like a doctor who wends his way through the crowds of a plague-stricken town. He who listens to the outpourings of a penitent soul in the confessional is like a doctor bending over an organism in which pulsate the living fibers of a departing life. Hardly less grave is the responsibility of the priest in his general action for the prevention of moral evil, or in his action on souls seeking for perfection, since a lost perfection may involve perdition. All this is no vain image; the priest acts on the real and on the mystical Body of Christ, in the Eucharist and in the Church. As an apostle, he acts on individual souls, and again his action is one of life and death. Weigh carefully all the consequences of this analogy and keep them ever before your mind, whatever may be hereafter the nature of the ministry committed to you.

I may seem to speak merely of the negative side of the influence of the apostolate, yet I in no way wish to disregard the fact that its positive element, which is to promote the growth of souls in their upward passage to Light and Life, is still greater and has much more bearing on the glory of God than its medicinal function. It is precisely in this that the originality of the Dominican apostolate stands out. It is also this aspect which wins and preserves for it its inviolable liberty. Yes, in order to draw souls to the Truth, and rally them to the command, "Walk as children of the light," the flame of our apostolate must burst forth through personality and action, free from all stains and trammels. Prepare yourselves through a manly practice of virtue to have the right to this apostolic liberty. In our Order the apostolic word is never hindered, except when we hamper ourselves with certain forms of good works which are outside our sphere and are perhaps even opposed to the genius of our Order. Your future liberty as apostles depends, in a great measure, on the ideal that you preserve of the apostolate. Remember that you have to deliver a sublime message, and to deliver it to the whole world. Narrowness, cowardice, routine, and still more a servile following of the fashion of the day, are the negation of the doctrinal and universal character of our Order. Certain easy successes are as real a bondage as inertia and ignorance. Yet I would sooner condone the impetuosity of those who throw themselves recklessly into the thickest of the fray, than I would those who spare themselves under the pretense of becoming champions and are not even good soldiers.

Let me conclude with a serious reminder: do not think that the masses of the people are incompetent to receive an intellectual message; experience proves that simple minds may be profoundly penetrated by deep dogmatic teaching, just as they may be reached by rationalistic propaganda. As the priest separates the Eucharistic Elements without any particle being bereft of the Divine Substance, so also the Dominican apostle ought to break the bread of the word and give it to the little ones without any crumb being bereft of the substance of divine truth.

IV

Veritas

The genius of the Order is Truth. To understand aright the words of Honorius III, Champions of the Faith (*Pugiles Fidei*), which I have already quoted, and of which we should never lose sight, we must interpret them by those words of St. Thomas concerning Faith: *Fides primo et principaliter in speculatione consistit, in quantum scilicet inhaeret primae veritati*—"Faith consists chiefly and in the first place in speculation, inasmuch as it cleaves to the First Truth" (Summa Theologiae, II–II.9, a. 3). We are dedicated not only to Truth, as embodied in articles of belief and the moral law, but to the very idea of truth as being the primordial character of the divine Life and of the Christian Revelation; the source of all moral law and holiness in the Church; and the fundamental reason of her authority and prerogatives. So we are bound, in virtue of our doctrinal mission, to present every object of our teaching in the first place as *true*; and our own lives ought to be governed rather by the influence of the true than even by the attraction of the good, and our external activity should appear as principally directed towards the diffusion of light.

First, let us try to justify from an historical point of view the intellectual and speculative character of our mission, and second, to express it in a more comprehensive definition, which we will take as the definite idea and device of the Order.

We can admit a distinction between the *idea* of a religious Order and its aim. The idea of a religious Order must, of course, coincide with its aim; its idea is nothing more than its aim seen from God's standpoint. An Order can determine its own aims, but we seldom see a founder put forth from the very first the divine idea of his foundation—for the very last thing a man is aware of is his own spirit. So the idea appears as something higher and almost independent of human legislation, a sort of inspiration, hidden—as inspiration generally is—and yet dominating and unalterable.

As time passes, it becomes possible to disentangle the idea of a religious Order, and we do it every day. For instance, we can formulate the Benedictine idea. The Benedictine Abbey is Christendom in miniature; it has the stability and autonomy of a city; it has the variety and the fullness of social service; it manifests the civilizing principle of Catholicism. The Abbey is the cell of the great Christian organism. The Benedictine Order is a form of spiritual feudalism, suitable to every age. Because Benedictines have been the initiators of Christian civilization they are also its archivists; they are the official witnesses of its history, the public notaries of its acts, and the custodians of its monuments.

Such is the Benedictine idea, and yet you never find it expressed in the Benedictine Rule, which only aims at making good monks.

The Society of Jesus seems to close the series of great foundations: it appears when Christian civilization is at the end of its ascendancy. Until then the Church, suzerain of Europe, was so intimately united to the life of nations that its means of defense were not only spiritual but material: Crusades, military Orders, the intervention of the secular arm, etc. But now the earthly city breaks off from the Church, sets up claims of Caesarian rights against the Church and of private judgment against spiritual authority. The consequent struggle of attack and defense was of quite a different order from that against barbarians and heretics in the Middle Ages. The Church had to hold her own on all the fields of social life. She had also to compete with the efforts of secular civilization. God then sent her a company of soldiers, admirably fitted for resistance and invasion, capable of brilliant maneuvers as an advance guard, and of self-sacrifice in the hour of retreat. The genius of the Company of Jesus is summed up in these two words: resistance and emulation. Hence its keen sense of the supernatural rights and interests of the Church; and hence also its character, at once both heroic and positive. This is why it is bound by a special vow to the Holy See, a vow that, though adding little to the canonical obedience common to all Orders, is a splendid bond between the soldier of Christ and the Commander-in-Chief of the Church. Yet, I wonder if a formal expression of this idea is to be found in the text of their Constitutions. Now it is striking that the Franciscans and Dominicans seem to have had a much earlier and a more explicit understanding of their respective ideals, although their founders were content to earn and deserve their titles rather than to formulate them. It is easy to understand that when a Catholic empire had been constituted by the spread of Benedictine colonies a new promulgation of its essential and vital law was a necessity. *Veritas* and *Caritas* are that law: from the time it was promulgated anew in the persons of St. Francis and St. Dominic it has persisted and will abide for ever. The contrast of these two types shows clearly that the mission of each is to be understood in a special and absolute sense; and though they were united as brothers, the difference between the ideas of their two Orders is wider than the difference existing among the innumerable modern religious, who, since the Council of Trent, may all be grouped under one type. Thus, the Dominican idea comes out from these historical observations and comparisons with sufficient clearness to give to the words of Honorius III a sense applicable *to* no other Order—a sense by no means metaphorical.

We can reach the same conclusion by taking another aspect of the same historical view. We said that the *idea* comes *from* God; let us now see what each Order renders *to* God, in virtue of its special predestination. It seems to me that, if the Benedictines represent the consecration to God of the principles of social life, the homage that by vocation they have to render to God is a family one, since Abbot means Father, and the Abbey is, as we have already said, the cell of Christian civilization just as the family is the cell of social life. Are not the Jesuits, at the other end of the coenobitic life, the representatives of the human will and of the moral character consecrated to God and controlled by the supernatural? In St. Francis it is the heart, with all its tender emotional power, with all its deep sympathy for nature and humanity, which is consecrated to Christ and marked with the impress of His passion. The Dominican homage consists in the dedication of the intellect to supernatural Truth.

All such homage rendered to God implies a sacrifice, so that heart, will, and intellect, each in its own way, fail not to suffer and be crucified. You need not be surprised if with us the discipline of the intellect is so severe, the method of training so rigorously and so continuously applied to all, if the integrity of our theological traditions is so jealously safeguarded, even by oaths, and if we are somewhat opposed to any form of mitigation or weakening in the intellectual sphere.

Moreover, that vocation of ours inevitably attracts emnities and persecutions. St. Dominic thirsted for a slow, piecemeal martyrdom, though (as the grace of persecution is a delicate one, which Saints do not abuse) he did not explicitly devote his sons to trials and sufferings. He left us liable to hard contradictions as we can see from the earliest times of the Order. *Veritas* is not always a recommendation to the world of today. We are reproached for pretending to an intellectual monopoly and dreaming of a scientific theocracy. It is no longer only the rule of Faith which is difficult to bear, but also the true rule of knowledge Many, especially among the young, turn from us through diffidence and fear. This is the more apparent and painful just now, in that, thanks to the glorious prestige of Père Lacordaire, we had been, at the moment of the restoration of our Order, everywhere greeted with an enthusiastic welcome. Happily, our vocation also wins the sympathy and devotion of many souls athirst for truth. Rest well assured that the world still expects great things from us, and that, if we are faithful, we shall see before many years have passed a band of chosen souls following the light of St. Dominic's star with the enthusiasm of those first sons of our revival in the nineteenth century, who hesitated not to apply to him the words, *Vidimus enim stellam ejus*—"We have seen his star."

From these remarks can we elicit a definite and comprehensive notion of the idea of the Order? This notion seems to me to be summed up in the phrase: *Fidelity to the Absolute*. Dante pictures St. Dominic as having from his very birth espoused Faith in the same way as St. Francis is known to have taken Poverty for his Bride: "When, at the sacred font, the espousals were complete 'twixt faith and him" (*Paradiso*, XII:61). Such an image implies not only absolute fidelity, but fidelity to the Absolute, as it is obvious that there is no fidelity where a single principle or consequence of truth is cast aside. Thus, we are bound to truth in its highest principles and in its ultimate consequences. This is the place to recall the words of St. Thomas:

"*Fides est assimilatio ad cognitionem divinam, in quantum per fidem nobis infusam, inhaeremus Primae Veritati propter seipsam, atque, ita innixi divina cognitione, omnia quasi oculo Dei intuemur.*" "Faith assimilates us to divine knowledge, inasmuch as through faith we adhere to the supreme Truth for its own sake, and so, upheld by divine knowledge, we see everything as if through the eye of God" (Commentary on the *De Trinitate* of Boethius, q. III.1, ad 4).

I am tempted to end with this beautiful text; I will, however, place before you some of its chief applications.

Very few people have even a faint idea of the Absolute, even in relation to morals. We sometimes in our ministry come across people who imagine that we can dispense from the commandments of God. In the dogmatic order, still fewer are able to perceive Truth in that august form which we term the Absolute. Some people, it is true, pronounce the name of the Absolute, but how dim is the corresponding notion in their mind. I would compare them to dogs baying at the moon. We are bound to more precision. The Absolute means to us: an object or a law of the intellect, firstly, free from sensible images; secondly, implying an intrinsic necessity; finally, universal in its necessity and truth.

The only end of our study and of our contemplation is to enable us to get a glimpse of absolute Truth just as the end of all ascetic and moral discipline is to enable us to have a foretaste of Absolute Good. Always, and in all things, we should exert ourselves to surpass the shadows and images, as says the epitaph of Cardinal Newman.

The Faith, of which we are the champions, by which we should live day by day, and which we have to spread abroad, is the Faith that sees all things as if through the eye of God.

How can we serve that sublime Faith if we let ourselves be carried away by that intellectual inconsistency which, in the name of life and action, sacrifices more or less the Absolute to that which is changing and contingent? The upholders of this tendency, if they do not deny the divine Essence and the reality of the contents of Revelation, are logically led to believe God conditioned by His creation, and to blot out from the Gospel the robust idea of the attributes of God. Such men suppress intellect in the name of life, as if intellect were not the highest degree of life. They really subordinate thought to sensation, and the vast heavens to our miserable earth. For example, William James (the specialist of religious experience) goes so far as to say that "we have to help God to do His duty"!

Fidelity to the Absolute is for us a promise of harmony and conquest even in the sphere of natural knowledge, not only because it preserves for us the indispensable health and precious energy of our mind, but also because the absolute principles held by us are so broad that they can embrace and reconcile in themselves the scientific conclusions of all ages. To that broadness of our principles Leo XIII, in his Encyclical *Aeterni Patris* (On the Restoration of Christian Philosophy), gives this splendid testimony:

> The Angelic Doctor has contemplated the philosophical conclusions in definitions and principles, which extend to the farthest possible limits, and contain in themselves the germs of almost infinite truth to be expounded at the proper time, with the greatest possible fruit. Having also used this mode of reasoning in the refutation of error he found in himself the means with which to combat all the errors of past times, and furnished invincible arms with which to repel those errors which will recur in ever-continuing cycles. (*Aeterni Patris* §18)

Fidelity to the Absolute is also a promise of triumph in our spiritual and even in our practical life. Many discerning people must have been struck by the freshness, innocence, and disinterestedness of those who have spent years in the study of metaphysics. When they come into the real world they hardly realize its faults, its hideousness, its sufferings, or its deceit. They seem to be quite oblivious of all the petty concerns of life. It is usual to look on the poet as the ethereal and splendidly unworldly man: I venture to affirm that the metaphysician is the true poet.

Some affect to suspect us of fanaticism; but, happily, serious historians are beginning to recognize the greatness of Dominican sincerity, even in the deeds of the most terrible of our ancestors. They point out that we had to do battle for the Church at a time when not only Manicheism but also Islam and the Greek Schism, through Frederick II, threatened to invade Western Christendom.

As to the practical spirit, St. Thomas seems to say that it is an extension of the speculative spirit. *Intellectus speculativus per extensionem fit practicus* (*Summa Theologiae*, I.79, a. 2). The speculative spirit becomes practical only by its own extension. The metaphysician judges with impartiality and patience, and in a single, brief principle he sees at a glance a multitude of practical consequences. Besides, being generous, the metaphysician uses the means of action without counting the cost.

To conclude, let us devote ourselves, body, soul, and spirit, to the service of absolute Truth. We must avoid the childish illusion of all kinds of liberalism. We shall not be the less sympathetic and human. In my opinion, Père Lacordaire enters more perfectly into the Dominican type in virtue of his wonderful sense of the Absolute and the Supernatural than even by his public influence and action upon the modern world. Remember, we are the children of light and truth: our Father St. Dominic was described to his most illustrious daughter, St. Catherine, in a revelation as an image of the eternal Word.

> Now, look at the ship of thy father Dominic, My beloved son: he ordered it most perfectly, wishing that his sons should apply themselves only to My honor and the salvation of souls, with the light of science, which light he laid as his principal foundation, not, however, on that account being deprived of true and voluntary poverty...but for his more immediate and personal object he took the light of science in order to extirpate the errors which had arisen in his time, thus taking on him the office of My only-begotten Son the Word. Rightly he appeared as an apostle in the world, and sowed the seed of My Word with much truth and light, dissipating darkness and giving light. He was a light which I gave the world by means of Mary, placed in the mystical body of the holy Church as an extirpator of heresies.

> Being clothed in faith, and hoping with firm confidence in My providence, he wishes his sons to observe obedience and to do their duty...Illuminated by me, the true light, he provided for those who should be less perfect, for though all who observe the order are perfect in kind, yet one possesses a higher degree of perfection than another, yet all, perfect or imperfect, live well in this ship. He allied himself with My truth, showing that he did not desire the death of a sinner, but rather that he should be converted and live...Of a truth, Dominic and Francis were two pillars of holy Church, Francis with the poverty which was specially his own, and Dominic with his learning. (*Dialogue*, Treatise of Obedience)

V

Preparation for the Doctrinal Mission of the Order

The apostolate of the Order is necessarily a doctrinal apostolate. It is to be remarked that with us preaching has always meant teaching, that is, of course, teaching of the Faith and everything relating to it, whether it be the foundations of Faith, or the consideration of the realities of those things of which Faith is the substance, or to the whole body of speculative deductions derived from revealed principles. Even when teaching morals, we do so in close connection with the first principles of ethics, following the masterly method used by St. Thomas in the second part of the *Summa*—principles which are themselves widely illustrated by, and inseparably connected with, Revelation. All preachers and teachers within the Church have perhaps a right to apply to themselves the motto from St. Thomas: *Contemplata aliis tradere*, to hand on to others the fruits of our contemplation, but it is obvious that it has always been applied to us in a more intensified and almost exclusive way. Still more striking is the fact that, although St. Dominic has never been officially proclaimed a Doctor, though he has left nothing

51

in writing, though we do not even know his method of preaching, yet he is hailed in the liturgy as having illumined the whole Church by his doctrine. (*Illuminare voluisti meritis et doctrinis.*) Men like Dante, who may almost be called his contemporaries, testify that this exceptional praise from the Church is called forth by Dominic's exceptional mission. The great poet sees in St. Dominic not only a great Doctor:

> For love of the true manna
> In short season he became a mighty Doctor.
>
> (*Paradiso*, XII)

But he calls the doctrine which he expressly attributes to St. Dominic—*Wisdom*:

> By his wisdom was on earth
> A splendor of cherubic light."
>
> (*Paradiso*, XI.)

Hence there is nothing equivocal in the exalted character of the doctrinal prerogative and mission of the Order. It behooves us to examine what this prerogative claims from each one of us.

It requires study, and the experience of things divine.

As to the study, you know how forcibly it is enjoined upon us, and what Cardinal Cajetan thought of a Dominican who studies less than four hours a day. This duty may be neglected in two ways: either by not studying at all, or by studying worldly things. The one leads to the other. Is such an evil unknown? Frankly, I think not. The taste for study is gradually lost through our own fault, and ends finally in an absolute inability to study. There are religious who never look into a book from morning till night, and sometimes even the periodicals which come into the community are cut only at the pages containing fiction. I fear that, as far as study is concerned, some of us may compare unfavorably with many men of the world, who never let a day go by without striving to improve the technical knowledge required by their professions, and keeping up with the discoveries and enlightenment of the day. It has been said that to know anything thoroughly you must have forgotten it seven times. There is no doubt that you must have learnt it more than once. It is the common experience of all of us. It is true even of a branch of study of such concrete and practical importance, for instance, as moral theology. But here I am speaking of the acquisition of knowledge in a higher sense, that is to say, of learning and habits of study in special relation to the universal character and mission of the Order.

In regard to this, let me say that at all times two tendencies seem to have existed among us. Some were inclined to devote themselves to study only in view of immediate spiritual utility. To them, knowledge was only a function of asceticism. They unconsciously reduced the use of books to what is in our day called spiritual reading, and were, by preference, drawn exclusively to ethical considerations. They were therefore liable to put aside abstract and dogmatic science, and still more to neglect information subsidiary to divine knowledge and the branches of learning connected with it. Of course, they were opposed to any form of what is called criticism; and they did not take kindly to any attempt at a scientific synthesis.

As regards Sacred Scripture, they were naturally interested in its spiritual meaning, in a way that almost excluded the literal sense, and that led them little by little to be absorbed in the accommodative sense, which is not a sense at all, and which may be found in any profane author.

I myself remember a superior in the Order who could not bear to see in the hands of his subjects any book relating to the New Testament except the Life of Our Lord by Ludolf the Carthusian. Some years ago an illustrious French Bishop was much praised for his clever adaptation of the words of Scripture to his own thoughts. One day a distinguished priest said to him: "My Lord, you are compared to Bossuet for your scriptural knowledge. Let me tell you that Bossuet assimilated Scripture to himself, you veneer yourself with it."

Needless to say, I have no desire to repudiate Ludolf the Carthusian, any more than I have the beautiful commentaries of St. Thomas or Hugo of St. Cher. To their rich theology, modern books can add nothing, but this is not to belittle the contributions of subsequent writers on other lines.

At the beginning of the nineteenth century we had in France a school of lay theologians, such as Joseph de Maistre and M. de Bonald, who, though ardent traditionalists, had as little taste for Scholasticism as they had for Criticism. Without going so far as these good men, we must be on our guard against influences and tendencies which might in some cases imply indifference with regard to Theology itself. I remember once hearing of a conference being given in a Studium of our Order, practically condemning study, under the pretext that "*Scientia inflat.*"

Fortunately, there is another tendency which may be called Aristotelian—or let us say truly Dominican—which bases the duty of study on the rights of natural and revealed Truth; which considers all the provinces of science as tributaries of Truth; and which seeks and finds in each of them the glimmer of that Light which enlightens every man that comes into this world. Those who represent this tendency are no more opposed to the experimental sciences, the archaeological and positive documents, than they are to the use of the deductive method. They will always refer their researches to the rules of logic, and ultimately to metaphysical principles, just as they refer metaphysics to Revelation.

There is a beautiful painting by Benozzo Gozzoli: St. Thomas seated between Plato and Aristotle, who stand on either side. There is also a famous fresco in Florence, showing St. Thomas completely surrounded by the Sciences, Arts, and Virtues. Both show that the doctrinal mission of our Order and the obligation of study were understood in the sense of that second tendency, which I maintain to be the true one.

When we find our primitive Constitutions allowing the study of pagan philosophy within limits— *"ad horam"*— this, considering the times, may be taken as a liberal concession; and the limitation implies that profane studies should be subordinated to divine science. We know that Blessed Jordan, the compiler of those Constitutions, in a letter describes with approval the attraction exercised by the Order, on "artists," men of science and letters, even more than on theologians.[†] You see then that study, in its most comprehensive sense, is an essential preparation for the doctrinal mission of the Order.

Now as to *experience*, which is the necessary completion of study. By experience, here, we do not mean any extraordinary intercourse with God, or any miraculous illumination, such as we find in the lives of the Saints, or such gifts as were the *"charismata"* of the early Church.

There is a kind of experience to which we may all aspire. It is something more than the joyful and strong feeling of conviction, something more than the sense of mastery a man may feel who has devoted his life to some subject. It is a serene apprehension, a real grasp—personal, complete, and overwhelming—of the sovereignty of the object of our faith and knowledge. Such experience, imperfect as it is when compared to the reality, is only possible with the grace of God: it belongs to the supernatural

---

[†]   Père Mortier, *Maitres Generaux*, I, p. 146. (Editor's note: *Maitres Generaux* is a work on the Master Generals of the Order of Preachers.)

sphere. It presupposes a negative condition, namely that our lives be not shut off from the light granted to us or acquired by us from revealed principles. It may be said that sincerity is the first step towards experience. Simple souls are rare and there are few indeed who have not a dual self and a divided personality: we all tend to lead a double life. It is only the generous few who do not impose on God a kind of concordat, which measures and limits the influence of the supernatural in their lives. If it is true that the habit does not make the monk, it is even truer that nothing should disguise the monk: he should appear always and everywhere in all things. Our obstructions before the inspirations of the Holy Ghost and the breaking up of our own self into many characters—these are the things that explain why we lack the experience of divine things, or at any rate why it is interrupted and weakened. Call it what you will, sincerity or generosity: only constrain yourselves to put your lives in harmony with your knowledge and faith.

When we study, teach, or preach, let our hearts and our wills follow the impulse of our mind towards God. When we study supernatural Truth, our reflections and conclusions of themselves lead us to the highest ideas of God, of His Life and attributes. In actual fact, we do not always follow them. They should, of course, carry us with them to the end of their flight, but we stop halfway; our affective power falls short of its aim. Thus, while we really possess the great principles which are the vantage points of wisdom, we lack the second element of wisdom which is the enjoyment and sweet tasting of the truth we contemplate.

When speaking of the temporal mission of the Divine Persons, St. Thomas says that the Divine Word is sent to instruct our intelligence in such a way that *"prorumpat in affectum amoris,"* it rushes into loving affection. Such a perception, he says, is properly called wisdom. It is the sweet savor of knowledge. He gives the reason for it in an untranslatable sentence: *"Filius est Verbum, non qualecumque sed spirans amorem."*[‡]

Let us never forget that all truth comes from the Son of God and returns to Him. So also our study must unceasingly bring us back to Him. When we have reached this experience and true wisdom, we no longer fear the wisdom of this world; we easily appropriate to ourselves all there is in it of good, and so the antinomy between the ancient and the Christian ideal of wisdom seems to find its solution. Those who do not know the supernatural source of this wisdom are tempted to give the honor to prudence, tact, and taste, and to see in this wisdom something borrowed from paganism. The following page, taken from Prof. W. M. Ramsay, is very significant in this respect:

> Paul never adopted that attitude of antagonism to philosophy, which became customary in the second century... On the contrary he says: "Regulate with wisdom your conduct towards the outside world, making your market to the full from the opportunities of this life. Let your conversation be always gracious, seasoned with the salt and the refinement of delicacy, so as to know the suitable reply to make to every individual"—the attic salt is here introduced into the sphere of Christian Ethics.... It is in Phil. 4 that his spirit is expressed in the fullest and most graceful and exquisite form: "Whatsoever is true..."
>
> We can picture faintly to ourselves the electrical effect produced by teaching like this on the population of the Galatian cities, on a people who were just beginning to rise from the torpor of oriental peasant life, and to appreciate the beauty of great thought and the splendor of Roman power. (*St. Paul the Traveller*, chapter 6,

---

[‡]   The Son is the Word, not any sort of word, but one Who breathes forth Love. (*Summa Theologiae*, I.43, a. 5, ad 2).

section 3.)

It would be more true to say that Paul the Pharisee had to learn from Christ crucified all his exquisite and divine virtues.

St. Dominic, like St. Paul, was a type of that wisdom which surpassed and included all that was refined in ancient ethics. Simple, humble, and poor as he was, St. Dominic stands out with such greatness because, in him, love came forth from light and was ever equal to it. If we belong to a school of divine wisdom, and if we remember that our essential duty is to spread abroad that wisdom, we shall be moved to ask of God—and strive to deserve—the experience of things divine, without which our teaching would be in vain, and the Divine Word entrusted to us cease to breathe forth Love.

"*Filius est verbum non qualecumque sed spirans amorem.*" "The Son is the Word, not any sort of word, but one Who breathes forth Love."

VI

The Canonical Character
of the Order

There are signs of a return among us to the idea that we are an Order of Canons Regular, an idea which seems often to have been thrown into the shade by our title of *mendicants*; yet the prologue of the old Constitutions, the Pontifical Bulls, and numberless other documents—even from non-Dominican sources—expressly call us "*Ordo Canonicus.*" It is true that in 1249 a general Chapter at Treves replaces the word *canonicum* by *clericum* in a passage of the Constitutions, but it is practically proved that this was only a means of defense against the hostility of certain university men, who wished to exclude us from the ranks of the clerics in order to prevent us from teaching. On this point we have not only positive textual proofs, but also the striking confirmation of such controversial documents as, for instance, *A Memoir on the Canonical Character of the Institute of St. Dominic*, published in France in 1750. In this sense we should understand the solemn admonition given by St. Dominic on his deathbed: "*In religione canonica perseverate*"† (Theodoric of Apoldia): he was not expressing a vague title, but a definite idea, which his own past

61

as a Canon Regular and his choice of the Rule of St. Augustine had inspired him to give to his Order. Let us try to justify the canonical character given to the Order from its very foundation by the precious advantages that it confers on our life and action.

In opposition to the modern opinion that dissociates the apostolic mission from the canonical state, we maintain the truth that the two are inseparable. We must get rid of the conventional idea of the canonical life, which to some minds suggests something humdrum, unattractive, and sterile. Such a notion is a caricature of the reality. The Apostles are the true types of the canonical life. We see in the Acts that not only did they go up into the Temple at the hours appointed for prayers (Acts 3:1), but that the first gatherings of their disciples were held in the porch of Solomon (Acts 5:12); and the sacred writer, as if to point out the religious and ritual character of those gatherings, adds, "But of the rest *no man dared to join them; but the people magnified them.*" Very soon afterwards, the Apostles are led by the practical difficulties of charitable administration to define explicitly the canonical character of their life in those well-known words, "*But we will give ourselves continually to prayer and to the ministry of the word.*" (Acts 6:4.) Here prayer means common and public prayer. So true is it that the life of the Apostles should be understood in this sense, that St. Augustine, when organizing for himself and his friends a life of common prayer, professes by that very fact to put himself under the patronage of the Apostles and to walk in their footsteps: *Coepit vivere secundum regulam sub sanctis Apostolis constitutam*—"He began to live by a rule drawn up according to the manner of life of the holy Apostles."

---

‡   *In religione canonica perseverate*: "Persist in right worship."

Therefore St. Dominic, in making us Canons, binds us to the primitive apostolate by a second tie. The Apostle, the preacher, is above all the man of God; his testimony must come, in one way or another, from his personal experience of God. He is the man of Mount Sinai and of the Holy of Holies: the sanctuary and the choir are for him his Sinai and his Holy of Holies. His whole life is regulated by the service he has to render there, and those to whom he is sent should see on his brow the sign that he is consecrated and is of the household of God. There is this difference between the Gospel type of apostle and all human imitations of apostleship: the sham apostle is a mere propagandist; the genuine Apostle is entrusted with a solemn message from the House of the King, which is to be delivered with due dignity. Thus, it seems to us, the canonical life is the countersign and guarantee of the authentic apostolate, and we owe it to St. Dominic's genius and foresight.

I hope I shall not be accused of exaggeration if I draw a conclusion that may seem to clash with the modern mania for an almost feverish activity. As I have already said, we are not made for all kinds of apostolic work, or rather, not for all that goes nowadays by that name. The true measure of our apostolate, and the true rule for discerning the nature of the work we should undertake, is that which safeguards, not merely the indispensable minimum of choral observance, but also the distinctive greatness and the substantial and life-giving fruit of our canonical life.

From what I have just said, we see that in the primitive Church canonical observances were not only the framework or background, but one of the principal sources and mainstays of the spiritual and mystical life; with us, too, it must be something more than an external frame or setting, it must be the very basis and root of our spiritual life.

The idea of the interpenetration of the sacred rites with the spiritual and mystic life is to be found, as one of his leading principles, in the writings of the pseudo-Areopagite, when he magnifies the powers of the ecclesiastical hierarchy so highly as to associate it with the heavenly hierarchy. Moreover, the comparison in the liturgy of the Church to the heavenly Jerusalem throws a new light upon the spiritual bearing of external worship. We can understand how in those early days the vigorous faith of Christians—for whom the veil that hides God was all but transparent—recognized in the sacramental rites the fullness of their supernatural reality and spiritual value.

Does it not sometimes seem that for us these great sources of grace have lost their freshness? The ceremonies with which the sacraments are celebrated have no longer the same symbolic eloquence; they seem stale and uninteresting to our jaded or over-excited natures. Few there are who see that the official prayers of the Church may take the place in their daily life of the ordinary devotional practices, that, for instance, Prime and Compline may be said as morning and evening prayers. Fewer still are wise enough to find in the Liturgy a refuge and a support in all the various circumstances of life, and a ready form of expressing all the diverse feelings of heart and soul. To such people the Liturgy hardly seems to be a prayer at all. We hope there is no truth in that story of the Provost of a certain Chapter who, when terrified by a sudden thunderstorm, held up the recitation of the office, saying "Let us stop and pray." The fact is improbable, but the satire is sadly significant. Still fewer are those who know how to find in the liturgical functions the grace of true contemplation; and yet the official praise of the Church should lead to nothing less than divine contemplation, since its first and direct object is the Blessed Trinity itself.

Omnis illa Deo sacra
Et dilecta Civitas,
Plena modulis in laude
Et canoro jubilo,
Trinum Deum Unicumque
Cum fervore praedicat.

Now, given that the canonical life is obligatory upon us, we must find in it all that the primitive Church found, and consequently not only the form of our daily exercise, but also the most efficacious of all systems of spirituality to help us to tend to perfection, from this source may be drawn even the highest gifts of the contemplative and unitive life. The proof that the canonical life is the dominating element in our own spirituality is that it seems to extend to the commonest details of our life, giving even to our simple daily meals the character of a religious ceremony.

The Liturgy extends into every department of our spiritual life: while externally it seems to complicate it, actually it simplifies our internal life in a wonderful way. I have nothing but pity for the religious, who, for instance, cannot find in the liturgical recitation of the *Confiteor* an occasion for renewing his contrition and making his examination of conscience—even his particular examination; who cannot see in the Superior's blessing the renewal of his obedience, in the inclinations the renewal of his humility, and on innumerable other occasions the exercise of perfect charity. I can only pity him who, after long years of religious life, finds in the choral office no gleam of light upon God and life divine. Let us remember that, in past ages, God seems to have preferred to grant His extraordinary favors in choir, during the liturgical offices, just as in the primitive Church the wondrous manifestations and mystical gifts of His Spirit were poured out during the liturgical celebrations. We can surely find in the choir

all good things; if we did but know it, the choir, attended faith-
fully day by day, is the source of our most precious graces. It
would be a calamity if we were found among those who do not
even seem to know what choirs are for. A Benedictine, not long
ago, was conducting a modern religious through his monastery.
As they passed through the cloister the latter exclaimed: "What a
nice place to say the Breviary." "We have a nicer one," the monk
replied. "Really, where?" "The Choir, of course." I may add that
the choir is not only fit for the Breviary, but is also the very
center from which our life should issue unceasingly and towards
which it should ever converge. The true theory of contemplation
unites liturgical with private prayer, the choir with the cell.

Our two great duties, study and teaching, far from being
impeded by our canonical life, are actually helped by it. The
Liturgy harmonizes them and completes them. If it is true, as
we have already said, that our apostolic mission implies a certain
judicial right, then our place is in the sanctuary, the doctrinal
judgment-seat. In ancient days the Bishop had his throne at the
very end of the apse, as if watching, both at once, the celebration
of the mysteries and the delivery of the word. We, too, have to
stand in choir as a judicial body. We stand there in choir not only
as canons performing a rite, but also, inasmuch as our doctrinal
office implies struggle and strife, like knights of old, who kept
vigil and dedicated their arms to God. But I will go further, and
venture to see in the canonical life a direct and living influence on
our doctrinal life. I think that study, begun in the cell, is perfected
in the choir; there, too, fructifies and ripens the preparation for
teaching in school or in pulpit. Speculative truths and moral
considerations take shape in the choral office as living realities;
they cease to be mere abstractions, inasmuch as for us the object of
study and teaching is identical with that of prayer: "*Lex orandi lex*

studendi." You know what is meant by mastery in any branch of knowledge: the ease of mastery stamps the true man of learning; he feels at home in his subject, he moves quickly through it, he is at once a daring explorer and an enlightened guide.

But when sacred science is in question it is almost impossible to reach that magnificent maturity without the help of liturgical prayer. During the Divine Office we gather up once more under familiar forms the sublime verities of our study; we are given a certain repose of soul for the fermentation, growth, and final assimilation of the truth within us. Masters and lectors have, of course, to use exemptions in the interests of their studies, but such privileges are not a break with that element of our life of which I am speaking. Whatever may be their personal knowledge, it would lack a kind of radiance if they systematically neglected to haunt the hearth of choral prayer. I am sure that halo of wisdom which marks learning in our Order is mainly due to the warmth and light gained in choral prayer.

Still less necessary is it to insist on the fruitfulness, for preachers, of choral office: how much empty vanity and superficiality, how much idle gossip would have been avoided if all preachers had been trained by the subduing yet ennobling discipline, by the mortifying and humbling exercises of canonical drill! St. Paul, greatest of preachers, most spiritual of ascetic masters, shows himself ever anxious about the perfect observance by the faithful of all the rites of public prayer; he seems even to conceive of private prayer principally under the form of a liturgical hymn: "*Speaking to yourselves in psalms and hymns and spiritual canticles, singing and making melody in your hearts to the Lord*" (Eph. 5:19). (See also Col. 3:16.)

We should feel grateful to God that we are able to establish historically the canonical character of the Order, and to affirm and repeat its essential necessity. The unanimity among us on this point is greater today than it was a few years ago; and I hope that a few years hence this lengthy affirmation of mine will appear to our successors the mere stating of an obvious truism. It was by a special blessing of God on the French Provinces that, shortly before their dispersion,[‡] perfect unity on this point reigned supreme. Blessed be St. Dominic for having enshrined all the rules of the ascetic and spiritual life in the canonical life of his Order. This is the real reason for the wonderful sanity and sobriety of our Constitutions on spiritual matters, which is in harmony with the sanity and sobriety of St. Thomas's writings on the same subjects.

There is no need to add that this sane outlook in no way implies lack of fervor and a complete grasp of all the content of the spiritual life. St. Dominic was not forced against his will and merely by existing circumstances to reduce the organization of our spiritual life to such simplicity. It was not the prohibition of the Lateran Council that dissuaded him from inventing a new rule and induced him for no other reason to adopt for his Order these traditional and apostolic features. The picture of him going from one side of the choir to the other, exciting his sons to sing more bravely and fervently the divine praises, symbolizes St. Dominic and his ideal. Our great danger is lest we forget, as well nigh happened in the sixteenth and seventeenth centuries, this necessary element of our life, without which we are neither Clerks Regular nor Dominicans. The private exercises of modern rules jar upon the great harmony of our lives. And why? Oh, why have we ever sacrificed to these intruders some of the finest portions of our daily canonical life? Let us increase and persevere in fidelity to the true spirit of our holy Father: "*In religione canonica perseverate.*"

[‡] This was in 1903.

VII

Liturgical Prayer

When we speak of Liturgical Prayer as an excellent and perfect prayer, as an exercise in meditation and even as a source of contemplation, two common objections are raised: (1) that it is purely vocal and too much a matter of words; (2) that it is too impersonal and not easily adaptable to individual needs. Let it be said at once that these objections are not serious. We may readily admit a certain incompatibility between private vocal prayer and meditation; but it is quite a different matter when liturgical prayer is in question. The choral hours, even when celebrated with the joyous briskness of Dominican custom, leave ample scope and full play for mental activity, in whatever direction that activity may tend. Besides, the divine praise—through the consideration of created things—goes straight to God: it fixes our attention firmly on the Supreme Object of our prayer. It is God we are concerned with, not the words, which are but the vehicle of our prayers. Thus the Liturgy makes it easier for us to transcend the facts and circumstances of our earthly condition; it enlarges the field of our vision; it leads us *per ea quae facta sunt* to the *invisibilia Dei*.

71

Liturgical prayer is, in a sense, like the double ladder of Jacob, by which we ascend and descend: that is why it implies an intense interior activity.

As to the second objection, there may be some particle of truth in it, but if liturgical worship empties us of self, that is no bad thing. The following considerations will show how much can be said for and against these objections. I will begin by speaking of the mental state which choral prayer requires from us, which I will call *the liturgical spirit*. Then I will go on to show how the sacred Liturgy raises the act of prayer to a wonderful degree of perfection.

The state of soul we describe as the liturgical spirit comprises several elements. It presupposes in us, in a certain degree, the acquired habit of prayer, and what is more, a profound knowledge of our Faith—I mean the great objects, the great monuments, and the massive doctrines of the Faith. Indeed, all the expressions used in the Liturgy offer in the fullest sense God's Revelation, since they are taken from inspired texts, in which Truth is presented under innumerable aspects and with an infinite possibility of moral application. Once the inspired texts have passed into the Liturgy there is no longer any question of the different senses of Scripture; one might say that, now that they fall *sub ratione Liturgiae*, we can use them to express whatever we would. They respond to our mood of prayer. They are endowed, as it were, with a kind of second canonicity—the fruitful source of a thousand mystical and moral meanings. So that it would seem to be an accurate statement to say that meditation is subordinate to choral prayer: the two are interdependent and by no means hampered or enfeebled by each other.

An equally important element in the liturgical spirit is docility to the molding power of prayer. I will readily grant you that the effects of liturgical prayer are not immediately apparent, for they must be won by patient training and perseverance. Those who will not or cannot overcome the instinctive reluctance felt by many modern people to joining in the Church's public, official prayer will never, of course, experience its priceless benefits. I maintain that, if you throw yourself wholeheartedly into liturgical prayer, it cannot fail to take possession of you, body and soul. It will color your thoughts with the varied hues of supernatural light, imbue your wills and your hearts with strength and love, and even stir your sensible faculties and your whole being, so that you will be able to cry out: *Cor meum et caro mea exultaverunt in Deum vivum*—"My heart and my flesh have rejoiced in the living God." If unhappily we seldom experience such effects in choral prayer, it is because, from the ingrained prejudice of centuries, we have been brought up to regard it as a dead or merely mechanical formality, good enough for musty old clergymen, but destitute of life or power to stimulate any but uncultured congregations. It is sad to see even intelligent people unable to understand the beauty of liturgical worship. How little they would understand us if we were to compare our Liturgy to the sacred dances of old. In order that the Liturgy may exert its molding power on us and establish order in our personality and in our life we must live in and by it. We must enter with sincerity into its smallest rites and seek the sap hidden in the least of its formulas. In this way the Liturgy will have a positive effect on our conduct and will lead us to practical resolutions and heroisms beyond our human weakness. While disengaging us from petty anxieties it will act on us unconsciously and mould us into greatness.

Though we cannot admit that liturgical prayer is unconcerned with our personal needs, yet we must lay stress on the fact that it transcends all personal considerations, the prayer is bigger than anyone engaged in it; and detachment and disinterested-

ness are the last and finest qualities of the liturgical spirit. May
we be permitted to say that in the Liturgy we merge our indi-
viduality into the supernatural life of the Church and become
one with her in her invisible action in the world? Or, rather is
it not more exact to say that it causes us to lose our personality
in that of Our Lord Himself? Bound as we are to choral prayer,
we become the living instruments of the prayer and praise of the
Church, the living echo of the life of the Glorified Humanity
of Christ. Have no wistful longings for the peace and quiet of
private meditation: the Liturgy throws open to you a door leading you into the joy of contemplation; you have but to enter in.
To follow that way is to follow the way of perfection, and in the
greatness of that way you will lose sight of self.

Even if the choral office could be separated from the Mass
we should still be able to say that it unites us to the intentions
of Christ and His Church; but the two cannot be separated.
The Divine Office is the prelude and preparation as well as the
setting and sequence of the Eucharistic Mysteries. Archaeologists
have traced the many relationships between the Divine Office
and the Mass. Indeed, our Matins present a striking analogy
with the night or morning service, held in the primitive Church
as a preparation for the Mysteries, such as we find it still in the
first part of Holy Mass as we now know it. The Psalms of the
Nocturns correspond to the *Introit* and *Gradual*; while in our
Lessons from the Old Testament or from the Epistles, in the
second nocturn giving the legends of the Saints, in the Homily
on the Gospel, there are relics of the Prophecies, the Apostolic
Messages to the Churches, the Acts of the Martyrs and the parts
of the Gospel which were read in those early celebrations. Then
the Catechumens were dismissed, and this *Missa* was followed
by the Holy Sacrifice. According to some scholars, the *Te Deum*

may be nothing else but an ancient kind of *Illatio* or Preface. This close dependence of the Breviary on the first part of Mass is at least a very plausible theory. (See *Illatio ou Te Deum*, by Dom P. Cagin.) Thus from its connection with the Divine Mysteries, and because it is the official prayer of the Church, the Divine Office leads us to unite ourselves with the purposes of God and the intentions of Christ and His Church. This is indeed another aspect of the fullness to be found in the prayers of the Liturgy; the fullness of intention. The four† ends of the Holy Sacrifice embrace in themselves all possible ends, which fall within the sphere of our Faith, Hope, and Charity. We can find them ceaselessly repeated in the Liturgy, like a kind of keynote which attunes us much more to the thought of God than all the details of our personal intentions. No greater sign of devotion to Our Lord and His Church can be given than the surrender of our personal interests and their absorption in the universal interests of God. The act of our prayer thus expands to the measure of the Church itself; it sheds its imperfections and its narrowness; it loses itself in the great harmony of adoration, reparation, petition, and thanksgiving, which rings unceasingly in the ears of God. Have you ever heard of that practice, dear to some modern souls, called the "heroic act," which consists in the abdication of one's merits in favor of the suffering Church in Purgatory? I venture to say that he who strives to identify himself with the intentions of the Church in the way we have described makes an equally noble act of disinterested surrender and becomes an even more generous and universal contributor to the welfare and glory of the whole Church of God.

After what I have said, I need merely name a third kind of plenitude, which, through the liturgy, brings the act of prayer

---

†   Adoration, Thanksgiving, Reparation, Petition.

to its perfection: I mean the plenitude of power or effect. Our personal intentions may be frustrated, but the intentions of Our Lord and His Church are certain of fulfillment, even if only in a mysterious and incomprehensible way.

For us, who are bound to the choral and public celebration of the Divine Office, there are surer guarantees of communion with the intentions of Our Lord and His Church than for those who have to content themselves with its private recitation. There always seems to me something of a parody in the private and individual, in the low-toned and almost silent use, of expressions essentially collective, for instance the simple *Dominus vobiscum*. It is to be noted that the Church has never exempted the individual priest, who says his Office alone, from these collective expressions, so there is reason to hope that she relies with greater confidence on those who carry out in reality the collective character of her prayer. She more gladly rests on their shoulders the burden of her intentions. Therefore, without presumption and without conceit, we may think that she recognizes in us the privilege of a special conformity with her spirit of intercession.

That spirit of prayer in the Church is the very breath of Christ's soul. When the Eucharistic Elements have ceased *to* be present within us there still remains in the soul an invisible influence of the soul of Jesus Christ: *Anima Christi sanctissima, sanctifica me.* What then could better preserve in us the precious power of that influence than the daily practice of liturgical prayer? Truly, in this respect, we can apply to ourselves, with a retouch which is but a development of their contents, the words of St. Paul: "I live, now not I, but Christ liveth in me." Truly we can say: "I pray, now not I, but Christ prayeth in me."

VIII

The Moral Character of the Order

The words St. Catherine heard from the Eternal Father: "The religion of thy Father Dominic is a delightful garden, broad, joyous, and fragrant,"† may be applied, not only to the rich and harmonious organization of the Order, but to its moral character as well. There need be no self-consciousness on our part when we set out to justify the greatness of the Order's moral character, since, after seven centuries of life, the moral countenance of an Order is presented to us as a well-established fact, neither fictitious nor fantastic. I will attempt to enumerate the qualities that make up our moral character, and I will set forth briefly the faults that imperil it.

In the first place, a sincere and impartial study of our past will bring clearly before us the Order's very real *nobility*.

By this I do not merely refer to its straightforward and disinterested spirit, as such, or to its share in the human and social glory of the Church during the thirteenth century, when the

Church's sovereign rights were accepted by the world; or to the prestige and charm of romance that our Order owes to its medieval origin—an age which, as a French writer puts it, had every failing except vulgarity.

I mean that a body of religious men is particularly marked with nobility, when its spirit is so brimming with life and so much a part of its essential life that it is transmitted, not as a heirloom, but as a vital heritage; when it holds and molds the individual, not by destroying any part of his perfection, but like the divine personality of the Incarnate Word, by lifting it up to a higher personality; when, in spite of differences of race and tongue, it creates a type infinitely varied and yet recognizable by a family likeness. To a religious body such a spirit cannot be infused from without, nor can it be the outcome of mere external regularity and formalism: it comes from the mysterious depths of some deep, distant, living spring. For nobility is in the blood, and comes from it; tradition cannot be made up on the spur of the moment; it is not anything that can be picked up or bought—a makeshift to be put on at will.

Now, such, I assert, is the spirit of our Order.

It is as clear as a vision to the greatest and to the least of the brethren; it acts as a stimulus upon each of us, and so strongly, at times, as to overwhelm us by its sublime energy, and to reduce us almost to despair of ever attaining its perfection. It identifies itself with the pure light of the absolute Truth, and yet it shines through the smallest of our rites and observances. It gives a lyric note to our life, and not only to the contemplative side of it, but even to our active life of strife and trial.

Again, a body of men can be considered noble, when its spirit is such as to raise its members to a certain level of greatness even with the great men of this world; with princes,

---

†   Treatise of Obedience in the *Dialogue*.

conquerors, social reformers, statesmen, discoverers, and all leaders of thought and action. Do not our golden age and the whole record of our history show our Fathers perfectly at ease, self-possessed, and serenely direct of speech, when they approach worldly dignitaries and the high and mighty of this earth? If other Orders can boast of having had many spiritual advisers and envoys at the courts of Popes and kings, our Fathers seem, in ancient days, not simply to have appeared as an occult influence in the Royal Courts of Europe or to have been mere candle-bearers, but to have held a place of dignity not only decorative but effective.

Perhaps the inner cause of this is to be found in the Order's unfailing devotion, not merely to truth, but to Truth Absolute, as formulated in principles. It may well be that between princes and principles of thought and action there is more than a verbal kinship.

We are even tempted to find another more remote and effective cause, foreshadowed in the Master's reply to Pontius Pilate's question: "Art thou a King then?" Jesus answered: "Thou sayest that I am a king. For this was I born, and for this came I into the world, that I should bear testimony to the truth." (John 18.) The *Ordo veritatis*, the Order whose mission is to be a witness to the truth, takes its rank among the royalties of the world.

Moreover, since nobility never falls away, but raises up all those who come within its influence, that group of men is noble whose spirit is endowed with the power to raise not only a few of their fellow creatures, but the mass of men, great or little, to a high degree of moral excellence, while remaining itself immune from cheapness and vulgarity. By almost a miracle of power the *Summa* and the Rosary have come from a single mind and soul: both are characteristically gifts of the Dominican spirit to what is loftiest and lowliest in the world. The *Summa* humbles the proudest minds by the sense of how little they can understand God's thought; the Rosary reassures the humblest minds by the sense of how little they can understand God's love.

No wonder so many noble souls have been conquered by the noble spirit of the Dominican Order. Before yielding to its attraction they often felt a dread lest it should be too noble for them; and when they joined it their craving for the "Mercy of the Order" was no cry of exaggerated humility. It is a plain truth that the Order is never ennobled by its subjects, however high their standing or however great their achievements; but they are ennobled by it. We have heard people say that this is even truer of our Order than of any other.

Keenness is another distinguishing quality of the Order. Here we may perhaps recall the symbol under which St. Dominic was seen in prophetic vision. Before the days of St. Dominic the dog was not of good repute, even in the Bible; indeed, it is almost excommunicated in the Revelation of St. John (Revelation 22). Its rehabilitation in the vision of Blessed Jane of Aza, in that feudal and hunting age, fits in with our description of the moral character of the Order, which implies a blind fidelity. At a mute signal the dog darts forth to defend his master and his house, to dash into the water or to fight. To his master he is attached passionately. Says St. Augustine, a great authority in favor of dogs: "*Vigilant enim et latrant boni canes et pro Domo et pro Domino, et pro grege et pro pastore.*" ("Good watchdogs keep guard and give tongue for the house and the master, for the flock and the shepherd.")‡

In a delightfully wholesome book, which tells the beautiful story of a dog, the devotion of the animal to his master is described in a few pages worth reading. "To the dog, first the

‡   Epistle 149.

man is the ideal master, then the dog has a trick of love-expression that is akin to hurt, and also he understands the oaths of his master to be love-words, and often his love is expressed in adoration."*

We might find every little touch and point of this picture in the history of our Order. Truth has taken possession of us as an ideal, has led us, at a signal of the Master, not only to the uttermost ends of the earth, but sometimes even to the violent extremes of difficult and terrifying service. Thus our spirit and our tradition are alien to such debasing compromises as religious liberalism (so called) and the false refinement of naturalism, which are only pusillanimity and cowardice in disguise.

Yet this thoroughness in the moral character of the Order is compatible with a glorious broadness of thought and feeling. Severe as our Order is, it is always guided by the principle that not the most difficult but the most true is the best. It demands from us a fidelity full of joy. It responds to the manifold aptitudes of men. I do not deny that our Constitutions and General Chapters sometimes concern themselves with details; but when they do so, it is because those details involve general principles. The fact remains, the spirit of the Order is neither small nor petty. It prefers to view things from the heights, and in their most sublime aspects. You know to what extent the spirit of our theological school, while giving to God the fullness of His rights, yet safeguards the integrity and perfection of human nature, and the completeness of a man's natural manhood. This we see in the saints and great men of the Order. In our history we sometimes come across what may be called a romantic element. It would seem as if Providence, as a counterpoise to the abstract and almost ruthless character of our doctrinal vocation, has, from time to time, given to the Order

---

* *The Call of the Wild*, by Jack London. Editor's note: This is a paraphrase of the particular passage, and not a direct quotation.

men whose personality was richer in sentiment, and whose life was more vividly colored than the classical type of the average. Let me mention, at the beginning of the Order, Blessed Reginald, who took Bologna by storm and died at the age of thirty-seven; then, in the domain of art, Fra Angelico; in the line of social action, Savonarola, Bartholomew de las Casas, and Père Lacordaire; in the sphere of mystical experience, Blessed Henry Suso and, to a certain extent, St. Catherine herself. Is not this the epic side of the history of the Order?

Also, the broadness of the Order appears in the living elasticity with which it allows itself like a living organism to be molded by circumstances, as we see in its origin. It is hemmed in, constrained, and impeded on all sides, yet it draws from those very circumstances its original greatness, its character, its rule, its distinctive complexity, its individual spirit. We are no opportunists, trimming our sails to this wind or that: we are no worshippers of compromise, that god or goddess of diplomatists; but we worship the Will of God; we believe in the supernatural and in God's Providence. This mingling of spontaneity and docility, this patient surrender to circumstances, combined with the wise control of them, is no small matter. Modern foundations have seldom displayed this double merit. They seek to extemporize a rule for themselves by reflective effort and by systematic and sometimes unfair appropriation. I remember hearing a nun say that she would very much like to have had the scapular as a part of her habit, but that "the nice idea had been judged impracticable." Even in this matter of the habit—now a most hallowed tradition in the Order—our Fathers characteristically awaited quietly the ordering of circumstances, and they were rewarded by receiving their scapular from the hands that spun the seamless robe.

The two dangers that threaten our moral character are cynicism and vanity. All our other possible faults may be referred to these two. Cynicism is the typical fault of the dog; not to press the application of this analogy too far, let me remind you that cynicism may come from a weakening of the moral sense, from laziness, or simply from sadness. Loss of our moral sense easily leads to contempt and to incorrigibility, which is cynicism in its deadly form. Though it is not absolutely unknown in the religious life, we will not speak of it here. The more common thing with us is to see the lamentable results of a continual disuse of our moral energies, a persistent cowardice which may lead to a depressed sadness and even to a kind of despair of ever attaining to the perfection of Dominican life. Soon, all resistance, all efforts, cease, and halfheartedly we resign ourselves to being below the level; finally, we settle ourselves into a definite attitude of failure, and publicly accept a position much more degrading than the most miserable mediocrity.

If trials from others supervene, if unkindness and injustice are added to our interior difficulties, then cynicism is tinged with bitterness and contempt, and in the end we believe neither in our own virtue nor in that of others. We hardly believe in the beneficence of the Divine Law, or in the reality of God's love. At this stage cynicism identifies itself with *acedia*.§ We easily understand the dangers of this state, which is quite the reverse of the dispositions of the Dominican soul.

At other times cynicism may be the outcome of scruples. Scruples are a frequent source of a kind of spiritual selfishness which is not easy to unmask, but when it does unmask itself it becomes impossible to root out and truly cynical. In such an egotist the field even of the spiritual life is limited to self-interest. Such a wretched soul makes itself the only center of all

---

§ St. Thomas defines acedia, or spiritual sloth, as "weariness in well-doing and sadness about spiritual things: it is an oppressive sorrow which so weighs upon a man's mind that he wants to do nothing" (*Summa Theologiae*, II–II.35, a. 1.)

the Order's great organization; its eyes are closed to the great currents of sin and error that spread over the earth. It cannot bring itself to understand that, if it is not permissible to save the world by the committing of a single venial sin, it is nevertheless monstrous to let it go to perdition rather than give up a petty practice, or step outside a little bit of devotional routine.

Cynicism is also a form of vulgarity. You will observe that, in the spiritual sphere, vulgarity either leads to or flows from practical unbelief: they both eventually become one and the same thing. By self-indulgence—to use a common phrase—we, as it were, *cut* God in some way; then we grow disgusted with His ways and manners in His adorable intercourse with souls; finally, we become incapable, not only of admiring, but of accepting as real, or frequent, or even possible, the wonders of His grace, such as fill the lives of the Saints. We say that we confine ourselves to the "*Credo*"; that it is quite enough for us and we forget that the *Credo* and Christianity itself and the commonest or simplest Christian life imply realities of infinite Love. Is this not spiritual cynicism? Is it less, or more common, than ordinary social cynicism in manners, tastes, and habits?

As to this last kind of cynicism (which is usually termed *bad form*), we all admit that the dog, faithful as he may be, is liable to it. Yet, although vulgarity may be compatible with a life substantially good, you will no doubt agree with me that at the present time it is a great evil, that it ought to be fought precisely in our democratic age more than ever before, and that it is an unbearable trial in our social life. Nor can one help admitting that vulgarity has its dire effects on our own mental and spiritual condition—that it leads to a lowering of the soul itself, to a want of tenderness in our relations with God, and to unfruitfulness in our apostolic ministry. There are, in the popular language, certain satirical nicknames tacked on to the different religious

orders; most of them are unfair and false, but we must beware
of ever justifying them or allowing them a modicum of truth
and of bringing them upon ourselves as a just punishment for
unfaithfulness to our religious ideal. For my own part I can
assure you that nothing pains me more than occasionally to hear
ourselves called "*Frati*" or "Frats" in tones of subtle and sinister
contempt and reproach.

As to vanity: it is with us a danger both for the preacher and
for the teacher. I do not say that in the preacher it is harmless; but
it is ridiculous, undignified, and unseemly rather than wicked.
God can turn to good the preacher's vanity as well as his incapacity. So you see I am not taking the ordinary commonplace
view which blames preachers for their vanity. I condemn vanity
much more strongly when it is systematic, that is to say when,
through vanity, the preacher lowers himself and his message to
the standard of the world, to the opinion of a particular place,
clique, or coterie.

When Dante puts on the lips of St. Thomas, among some
vehement reproaches against degenerate Dominicans, this
significant description of the Order: *U'ben s'impingua, se non
si vaneggia*—("Where well one fattens, if he strayeth not")
(*Paradiso*, X:96), I do not think he is specially referring to the
preachers. Such words bring back forcibly the words of St. Paul:
"They are lost in their vain conceits," and they seem to indicate
that he is rather thinking of those who are dedicated to learning.
When these latter yield to vanity they much more quickly fall
into spiritual pride; they are led into hardheartedness and dryness
of soul. They no longer perceive the limits of their knowledge,
make no further progress, and think themselves the oracles of
the world. Entrenched in their privileges, they have no conde-
scension for the needs of others. The exercise of charity is a work
beneath them and finally these learned men are incompetent to

catechize children. You know how severe a satirist Erasmus was for many of the doctors of his day. I have come across a legend apparently older than the writings of Erasmus and still more severe; in it masters and superiors of every degree are seen, in the room of a Neapolitan priory, burning with flames of Hell.

Let us turn our thoughts from these sad travesties of our moral character. Its true symbol is our holy habit, with its twofold hue of black and white, for penance and purity, and its double aspect of seriousness and joy. All these qualities make up the features of our character. Let us honor our habit even more highly than the soldier honors his uniform: it is indeed a splendid image and a holy thing. Let it be poor but spotless. I hate to see our habit the subject of those vulgar caricatures, unfortunately common in this country; and it seems to me shameful for any of us to laugh at them. Let our habit remind us of the character of our Order, and let us strive jealously to approach daily more and more to Dominican perfection. We can bear persecution and insult, but we must face even death itself rather than through any fault of ours allow our Order to be justly scorned.

IX

The Dominican Note in the Dictates of Our Conscience

There is something fine in the way St. Paul proclaims the great importance and value before God, though not the independence, of the human conscience. He says that whatever does not proceed from conscience, whatever is not in conformity with it, is sin. This statement contains something of a psychological mystery, for although conscience may be misinformed, yet we are obliged to follow it. Now although St. Paul admits, especially in practical matters and in doubtful cases, the decisive power of conscience, and although he is ready to grant that a man may be in good faith, yet at the same time in error, still he does not teach that everything which proceeds from conscience is really the voice of God, but only that which proceeds from conscience duly and properly instructed. At one and the same time, St. Paul recognizes in conscience a certain autonomy and yet he also realizes the obligation upon conscience of watching over its motives. Now, without pretending that our conscience differs from that of other men, I maintain that there is a special note, a Dominican accent, so to speak, in its dictates. I should like to show: (1) how nobly it guides us; (2) what are its chief motives and how to keep watch over them.

Although at every hand's turn and at every moment we find ourselves confronted with precise rules and regulations, yet a characteristic feature of our legislation is its respect for individual responsibility. To begin with St. Dominic—there is not the slightest doubt about the firmness with which he exercised his authority, yet he does not rule with a rod of iron, but allows scope among those who obey for a certain freedom and spontaneity. Thus, in 1219, in face of the difficulties over the transferring of the Sisters from St. Maria in Trastevere to St. Sisto, we see him releasing the nuns from their promise, and asking for a free renewal of their profession. Still more remarkable is the fact that, when obliged by Innocent III to rally his followers under one or other of the ancient Rules, he never dreamt of making his choice without consulting his brethren; the primitive chronicler does not attribute the selection to him alone, but to a collective and unanimous decision. Finally, this respect for individual responsibility is attested, signed, and sealed for all time by St. Dominic's refusal to bind his sons under pain of sin to the observance of the Constitutions. Such a spirit, which is the glory of the ancient monastic foundations, implies a perfect relationship between superiors and subjects. The absolute honesty of the subject should always be presupposed in the rulings and decisions of authority. Suspicion is quite alien to our spirit. Authority ought not to have recourse to a petty diplomacy in order to obtain obedience, but should openly appeal to loyalty, to supernatural motives, and to the religious responsibility of the subject. Still less should authority fall back on that system of governing employed by some modern politicians in order to rule their majorities, which we may term the government of men through their passions. Nothing is sadder than to see a superior who lacks the courage to ask straight out from his subject an effort or a sacrifice in the name of obedience. It is indeed a bad lookout for the community, and is very often the first step towards its downfall. Where such a state of things exists, the subjects, instead of congratulating themselves on being spared, ought to feel themselves degraded and put to shame.

The superior who gives credit for generosity in his subjects calls forth confidence from those he rules. Remember, it needs as much nobility of mind to trust as to inspire trust: suspicion is just as unbecoming in the subject as it is in the superior. Confidence sums up all the dispositions of the obedient mind: trust is the last blossom and crown of obedience. I do not deny that confidence may be sorely tried. But even the defects in authority can often be overcome by the persevering and unanimous confidence of the subjects. One may ask whether the dissolution of common life, through disunion between superiors and subjects, comes about through the fault of the former or of the latter. There is not the slightest doubt that, in the majority of cases, the subjects are to blame, if only for this reason, that the superior, being elected by them, ought never to be utterly discredited by them and treated as a pariah. The subject who acts ignobly at the end of his superior's term of office is quite capable of acting ignobly at the election of a new superior. Never let us allow bitterness and discontent to grow in our hearts. We should have the courage and humility either to stifle our feelings or else to express them with filial respect and then keep quiet and do our duty. If we do not act thus we are in danger of falling into the vice of servile obedience. The severe censure of St. Paul against "serving the eye" is not for us, nor is there any need to warn you against it. The principle of dispensation, so forcibly expressed in our Constitutions, which happily balances and tempers the complex and difficult elements of our life, is also, or at least ought to be, to us, an original principle of nobility in our conscience. In this respect the important thing is to use and not to abuse. Just as refinement of taste consists mainly in not insisting, so refinement of feeling consists in not abusing. For the majority of people it must seem the more obvious and, in a sense, the easier way to be men of extremes and to go the whole length rather than to keep to the ideal rule of moderation. At first sight our rules may appear extremely rigid, but dispensation, to which I have referred, is as much a part of our Constitutions as any of our other laws and of equally general application. Even when the superior takes the first step in dispensing, a great share of the responsibility still rests with the subject. If he is not so perfect as to feel positive suffering in using a dispensation, he must at least use it with tact and delicacy and with a spirit of mortification. The principle in our conscience that corresponds to the large and generous principle of dispensation, is a willing adaptability to this or that measure of dispensation or restriction. It is obvious that we may have to pass from one environment or sphere of activity to another, from one country to another, from this function to that. We must bring to these changes an equanimity, a self-forgetfulness which comes from true nobility of soul, a self-subduing force rather than a mere negative acquiescence and indifference of will. The more dispensations and privileges a religious receives, the less he should take root in them. Nothing is less easy to bear gracefully than the exceptional; it is in the use of exceptions that a man's true worth is made manifest. Noble natures are simple in the exceptional, and uncommon in common things.

In order to pick out the distinctively Dominican note in our conscience, we must examine the motives which chiefly weigh with us and are part and parcel of our lives. Our long metaphysical training not only enriches and strengthens the mind, but also primarily gives us *the sense of order*.

We are perpetually occupied in establishing the exact definitions of things, in formulating their laws and relations: thus we develop orderly minds; we put order into our ideas and our ideas into order. Thus we seize the meaning of St. Thomas's words: *"Ordo pertinet ad rationem sicut ad ordinantem"*—"Order belongs to reason as to its cause" (*Summa Theologiae*, II–II.26, a. 1, ad. 3). Now conscience, which signifies the habit of first moral principles,[†] is a function of reason and therefore it should normally follow the development of reason. It should display order in itself and it should put order into our moral life in proportion to that life's development. The idea of order should attract us for its own sake; it ought to be the beacon of our intellectual and moral life. It must be, in truth, the frequent object of our contemplation, since it bears in itself all the beauty of Platonic ideas and the depth and precision of Aristotelian concepts. We should have no concern for anything that is out of place, whatever be its charm or its material value. Any willful violation of order should repel and disgust us. We use the term *monstrosity* for certain exceptionally grievous moral transgressions: indeed, any violation of the essential order of things holds its place in the scale of monstrosities. Such a love of order is the first requisite for a healthy condition of mind and conscience; it constitutes intellectual honesty, right-mindedness, and moral integrity.

Such a conception of order, held by the mind and loved with the will, gives to our conscience its true Dominican character. Since, according to St. Thomas, order always relates to a

---

[†]   The habit of first moral principles is called by St. Thomas, *synderesis*, the act of which is to dictate in general that good must be done and evil avoided; whereas conscience dictates what must be done here and now in a particular case.

principle (*Summa Theologiae*, II–II.26, a. 6), it follows that whenever a principle, either logical or causal, is imperiled, we must fly to defend it. Zeal for supernatural principles is the highest form of justice and the highest motive of conscience. Is not this a distinctive feature of the Dominican conscience? We hold that principles are imperishable and are supremely worth dying for.

The sense of discipline, which is also an important motive of conscience, derives equally from the sense of order, or rather is its elementary application. When obedience is closely linked with the fundamental and supernatural sense of order, then it reaches its perfection and becomes in reality the *rationabile obsequium*—the reasonable service—which makes us not only obedient to the law, but also docile to the spirit of the law. The sense of discipline also trains us to believe that we have something to learn from others, and prevents us posing as originators or inventors. Among us, on the contrary, the sense of tradition prevails. Loyalty to the Church and reverence for her ancient Doctors are distinctive features of the Dominican conscience.

Finally, our love of order produces a willing subordination of our individual interests to the general law and to the common good. St. Thomas says that order, as to its subject, belongs rather to charity than to faith: "*Ordo magis appropriatur charitati quam fidei*" (*Summa Theologiae*, II–II.26, a. 1, ad. 2), that is to say it is the function of charity to carry out the subordination of different kinds of particular good to the common good of all and of minor laws to the general and supreme law. This is the vital motive of conscience that leads us to our essential and supreme end—the perfection of charity. Now it seems to me that the maintenance of charity first in its *appreciative* and then in its *intensive power* is a characteristic of our doctrines and of our asceticism. Hence the insistence amongst us of the teaching of St. Augustine in the Rule: *Non propria communibus, sed communia propriis praeferantur* ("the common good is to be preferred to our own private and merely selfish interests"). To bring these considerations to an end, let us be deeply grateful for the spirit of our Order and thankful for the doctrinal training we receive in it. The Dominican spirit, if we are but faithful to it, imparts true greatness to our conscience, and our training gives manly strength and a lofty elevation to our motives. So, little by little, we tend to realize in our lives those words of St. Augustine which express the ultimate perfection of conscience: *Ille juste et sancte vivit, qui rerum integer aestimator est*—"He is just and holy who sees things whole and estimates everything with a wise sense of proportion" (*De Doctrina Christiana* (On Christian Teaching), XVII.28).

X

The Turning of the Soul
to God by Charity

If the act of sin is a turning away from God (*ratio culpae consistit in aversione a Deo*), the act of charity can, on the other hand, be but the turning back to God. Note how striking an image these words contain of the movement of the human soul towards the Infinite Good. It conveys the idea of a spontaneous motion like that of a flower to the sun, and also a turning away with more or less of painful effort from the things of earth. There is in effect in us a deep and indestructible appetite for good, surpassing all the joys that come from things created. Outside the supernatural order that appetite remains an interested, or at least a vague desire, and a melancholy prerogative of our nature. St. Thomas describes it in these words: "Man has a natural appetite to be complete in goodness" (*De Veritate*, XXII.7). But, in the Christian, it becomes an act supremely intelligent, generous, and free. Yet it must not be a luxury, or a poetic element in his life, it should be the positive norm and ruling power of all his daily actions.

On this important point let me briefly remind you of a

few considerations, inspired by our traditional doctrines and eminently suitable to us.

You know how St. Thomas exacts from everyone who reaches the age of reason, a deliberate act, which directs his whole being to his last end. He goes so far as to attribute to that act the power of blotting out original sin; and he declares its omission to be a mortal transgression (*Summa Theologiae*, I–II.87, a. 6). Without entering just now into all the explanations that the text demands, we may note what a great idea he gives us of the initiation of the rational life in man. Our Christian education, implying as it does many acts of spontaneous dedication to God, reassures us on this vital matter of having chosen rightly, yet at the same time these words of St. Thomas carry us back to our early years and lead us to search anxiously for that solemn moment when we first turned to God. Whatever may in fact be the result of our search, we finally feel drawn to renew more consciously that act of loving dedication.

Our Lord, as man, dedicated Himself to His Heavenly Father from the first moment of His existence, and it may well seem that, in Him, that initial dedication needed no repetition. Yet, at the beginning of His public life, in the scene of the Temptation, we see Him give us the example of turning away from all the kingdoms of earth—not that temptation was a necessary trial for Him, still less was it a danger; but in that scene we have a solemn lesson, and we see the triumph of charity at the age when man reaches the perfection of his rational life. Still more for us is renewal of that act a necessity, for, as time goes on, the age of reason renews itself; at various periods our judgment changes, governed by the experience of life. As we advance towards maturity, and still more as we advance towards death, our horizon grows wider, the light thrown on our responsibilities grows clearer, the greatness of the graces we have received is made manifest to us, and it is impossible for us not to feel impelled to renew, in a more perfect way, our engagement with God. Recall one by one the events of your religious life and you will probably see that each called for a renewed effort towards the perfection of charity. But never think that it is too late to reenlist, I mean to renew your dedication to divine charity. One may be tempted to look back with regret and longing at the days of youth, to feel that the freshness and strength of devotion are gone, that the ideals of the past can no longer be realized. Oh! I beg of you, put these thoughts away: remember the words of St. Paul, who bids you "forget the things that are behind, and press forward to those which are before" (Phil. 3:13). Take in your hands the fruits of your maturity and offer them to God; take the strength of your manhood, the experience of your age, and dedicate them to Him. Press forward, constrained by the love of Christ. The charity of your youth was like water from a fresh spring, let the charity of your manhood be as wine from a vine in which flows the strong life of Christ Jesus.

An act of charity, such as we have been considering, impels us to tend to God as to our last end and to seek to embrace Him. But even this does not decide nor exhaust the question of the turning of the human soul to God. Many souls would think it foolhardy to attempt to embrace the Sovereign Good; they do not find in their hearts enough intensity of love to dare to claim for themselves the strong words of the divine precept: "With all thy heart, with all thy mind, and with all thy strength"; they would like first actually to realize that they have indeed cast under their feet all unworthy affections and all ignoble attachments to this world; they would like to feel their soul overflowing with desire, and their heart bursting within their breast. But are these feelings really necessary? No—such an intensity of feeling, even if it exists, is rare and exceptional. There are few seraphs on earth, and even those few remain, thanks be to God, most of their lives, men of common sense, men like their fellows. The intensity of charity is not to be despised, it is to be aspired to: indeed from the moment when "charity was poured out into our hearts by the Holy Ghost" (Romans 5:5) the key of the way that leads to it is already in our possession. This is the *appreciative character*, which is essential and formal in the supernatural habit of charity.

Appreciative charity means a positive preference for God above all else because He is the Supreme Good, and a readiness to give up everything for Him when asked. This seems to simplify and make easier the precept of charity. Still, we must not rest in this explanation. The sincerity of this preference needs constant watching, to prevent its reverting to a mere abstract and negligible principle. Therefore, we must ever be ready to test its effectiveness. We must ask Our Lord, like St. Paul: "Lord, what wouldst Thou have me to do?"— Lord, what wouldst Thou that I should offer and renounce for Thee? When, in the Divine Office, we meet such words as these: "My heart is ready, O Lord, my heart is ready," we can always echo, if not in exultation, at least with the certitude that we are expressing the sincere desire of our hearts. "Thy Will be done" is the sure test of our charity. The true and only kind of intensity by which, as St. Thomas says, charity can be increased (*Summa Theologiae*, II–II.24, a. 5), is that of good works and virtuous acts. The more fervently we act, the more lovingly we do the Divine Will in God's own way, the more we are rooted and founded in charity (Eph. 3:17). For, let us remember, the will, and not the sensitive appetite, is the subject of charity. Let us keep ever before our eyes the teaching of our Master: any act of charity prepares us (*disponit*) for an increase of that virtue; but charity is actually increased only by acts more fervent, "Each act of charity disposes to an increase of charity, in so far as one act of charity makes man more ready to act again according to charity, and this readiness increasing, man breaks out into an act of more fervent love, and strives to advance in charity, and then his charity increases actually" (*Summa Theologiae*, II–II.24, a. 6).[†]

Thus it appears that the appreciativeness of charity is not devoid of at least an initial measure of intensity. The contemplation of the Supreme Good, in God, is impossible without some emotion of the heart, some rapture and fervor. Anyhow, it is for us, whose doctrines have always affirmed the subordination of the will to the intellect, a special duty to let the luminous principles of the divine science produce in our souls both warmth and strength. For that we must open and unfold all the receptive faculties of our minds to the pure light of these principles. The sense of intellectual light and the love of absolute beauty, innate in us, need developing. Generally, they imply training and practice, and involve persistent effort. The perfect law is to seek intensity through appreciation, to go to love through light: so, if appreciative charity seems to some too cold, or if some are inclined to consider it unworthy of God, it is either because they have never, in real earnest, applied their minds to the idea and the contemplation of the Supreme Good: or because, on the contrary, they have studied the divine truths as they would any ordinary subject; and, through irreverent familiarity, have been refused the grace to find in divine science the fuel of divine charity. It is in that sense that Blessed Jordan said that theologians are sometimes like sacristans, who end by passing before the Altar without genuflecting. Dante is in full harmony with our doctrines when he speaks of divine charity as being kindled by the light of Grace:

[†]   *Quilibet actus disponit ad charitatis augmentum, in quantum ex uno actu charitatis…homo prorumpit in actum ferventiorem dilectionis quo conetur ad charitatis profectum: et tunc charitas augetur in actu.*

> Since   with   its   beam
> The grace whence true love lighteth first his flame,
> That after doth increase by loving. (*Paradiso*, X:83.)

> (*Lo   raggio   della   grazia   onde   s'accende*
> *Verace amore, e che poi cresce amando…*)

It might appear to some that I have not dwelt enough on the effective side of charity. If it were so, I could easily complete what I have already said. St. Thomas teaches that the mode of the virtues (which means, as you know, an ease, a firmness, and a joy deriving from their habit) is not, generally speaking, included in the precept; yet St. Thomas says that the mode in the practice of virtues "is the end to which the legislator intends to lead." (Ia–IIae, Q. xcvi, art. 3.) Hence the mode of virtue, while not being obligatory, is yet desirable: this is not a contradiction.

For "the charity of Christ constraineth us" more urgently than ordinary Christians, since we are bound to tend to its perfection: we cannot afford to think lightly of the end of the legislator.

> The perfection of charity to which the counsels make us tend, stands midway between the perfection of Heaven and the perfection of this life…and it consists in man's renouncing as much as possible temporal things—even those that are lawful, because they take hold of the mind and hinder the actual movement of the heart towards God. (*Summa Theologiae*, II–II.44, a. 4, ad. 3)

Is it possible to *stand midway between earth and heaven* without a higher flight of virtue on the wings of charity, without absolutely conforming our ways to the ways of Eternal Life, in which effort is unknown and joy reigns supreme?

I do not know any greater incentive to the practice of all virtues than this doctrine. It shows and asserts the commanding power of charity upon our lives. In plain words, it means that we should try not only to elicit acts of virtue but also to reach before we die the firmness, joy, and constancy of their *habitus*. Our vows themselves are only means to this end: the vow is practically for nothing but that. Fidelity to our spirit and vocation, earnestness, generosity, efficiency in the spiritual sphere, all consist in knowing it and willing it.

Moreover, that readiness of heart to do the Divine Will, which belongs to the very essence of charity, together with the obligation for us religious of tending to the fullness of the *habitus* of virtue, and not to elicit acts only, both imply a "preparation of the soul," as St. Thomas calls it, still more comprehensive and generous, to translate into action our preference for the Sovereign Good.

There are in the Christian life certain precepts and virtues which do not exactly compel us to exceptional acts, but require that we should be prepared to accomplish them when opportunity occurs. Such precepts, as that of "turning the other cheek," cannot be of universal and perpetual obligation, and such acts might often, out of due season, be unreasonable. Still, extraordinary as these precepts may be, when they are demanded by Divine Providence, they become simply reasonable, as St. Thomas says: *Ut scilicet, superveniente tali casu, homo secundum rationem agat*—"Then, not only reasonable are they, but obligatory" (*Summa Theologiae*, II–II.128, a. 1).

This *praeparatio animi* is a more real test of the true intensity and perfection of charity than jubilant transports of devotion; and note well that it has no other limits than those imposed by the Divine Will and the Divine Love.

Since ordinary Christians are not to be afraid of it, let us face it as far as it goes, let us keep it explicit, resolute, and joyful in our hearts.

I hope I have said enough to justify those beautiful words of St. Clement of Rome: "The heights to which charity raises us are unspeakable. There is nothing mean or sordid in charity" (First Letter to the Corinthians, 49.)

I have insisted on the dependence of charity on the apprehension of the Supreme Good, as revealed to us by faith, because this emphasizes the nobility of supernatural charity. In Heaven charity has its source in vision, and its consummation is in the possession of the Supreme Good, as Dante says:

> Light intellectual, replete with love;
> Love of true happiness, replete with joy;
> Joy, that transcends all sweetness of delight.
> (*Paradiso*, XXX:40)

> (*Luce intellettual piena d'amore,*
> *Amore del Vero Ben pien di letizia,*
> *Letizia, die trascende ogni dolzore.*)

XI

How a Dominican
Should Go to Confession

Penance is one of the distinctive marks of our Order. It is quite natural for us to associate this penitential side of our life with the precept of penance so strongly insisted upon in the Gospel, but in practice we do not always sufficiently connect our special obligation of penance with the Sacrament which bears that name. Nevertheless, contrition is the first source of penance, and nowhere is contrition deeper or more efficacious than in the Sacrament of Penance. If the illuminative, and even the unitive, life derive their force from this Sacrament, may we not say that the purgative life absolutely depends upon it?

Yet we should strive to draw from the Sacrament of Penance, not only all the perfections of the purgative life, represented by our penitential observances, but also a real growth in the spiritual life.

We begin with contrition. For a Dominican, contrition should be, above all, intelligent. We read in the book of Job: "To depart from evil is understanding" (28:28.) This understanding is rarely found among men. Theologians tell us that if man can urge any excuse for his sin in this life, it is that his changeable

109

and too easily distracted mind can scarcely so much as conceive of the idea of the Sovereign Good and still less hold It fast as the object of its preference over and above all else; hence in every human sin there is some element of error, a mistaken judgment. Far otherwise was the sin of the angels, who, in their willful and evil choice of a created good, acted from the first with completely enlightened understanding and with conscious and exact deliberation. But for human beings—since sin is the turning away from the Sovereign Good—a positive effort is needed even to understand the nature and gravity of a sinful choice.

In some ways the mere possibility of sin must ever remain a mystery. If God is the Supreme Good, why are we so little attracted? And again, even if we know but little of the goodness of God, should not that little be enough to ravish our hearts and convince us of the absurdity of sin? We outrage the Supreme Good, we offend God, we sin against God—these are terrifying thoughts; but *why* and *how* such actions are possible is beyond our power to explain, and the painful problem only deepens into a darker mystery when viewed in the light of the Incarnation and the Redemption. That the Son of God should have died upon the cross to destroy sin and yet that sin should be so little destroyed—that sin should be still so much alive within us; there we have the profoundest of mysteries, the absolutely incomprehensible. Yet incomprehensible as it is, the fact remains that sin is really an outrage against God and we must strive to convince our minds of the awful reality of that outrage.

These reflections lead us inevitably to remember and hold fast to the simple truth that contrition is supernatural. By the light of revelation alone, we attain the idea of the Sovereign Good. Faith teaches us that it profits us nothing to gain the whole world if we lose the Supreme Good. We are taught to have recourse to the passion of Our Lord as the source and motive of contrition. We cannot do this if we separate from the passion the idea of sin which is its cause, and if, in the Person of the suffering Christ, we do not see the God whom sins offends and the Sovereign Good from which sin turns away.

It is no empty notion of mere philosophical sin that I preach to you. Our aim is to point out that the Sacrament of Penance is an opportunity of knowing more clearly and of fortifying still more the intellectual grounds for our aversion from sin.

Beyond the pale of Christianity the definition of sin as a *turning away from God and a turning to the changeable good* (*aversio a Deo, et conversio ad commutabile bonum*) is either unknown and unintelligible, or is debased into a false and pessimistic mysticism. Even with us a serious applying of the mind is necessary in order to give these fundamental principles and definitions their full value and to draw from them all the energizing force which they contain. Here again we must remind ourselves of the doctrinal character of our Order; contrition, such as we have tried to describe it, is only a further illustration of the harmony which should reign between our study of truth and our spiritual life.

The second point, no less important, is the matter of the Sacrament. Obviously any grievous sin against our vows, which we should have had the misfortune to commit, provides necessary matter for confession. No need to insist on this. But the vows do not contain everything. Each vow has a corresponding virtue, which extends much further than the vow. Different souls, equally faithful to their vows, show marked differences in the degree of their perfection. The binding-force of the vow comes from the vow itself, in so far as it is sanctioned by the Church; but the binding-force of the virtue derives from another principle, namely from our obligation of tending towards perfection. This principle also carries with it the obligation of practicing many virtues other than those connected with our vows—in fact *all* the virtues, and we are bound to practice them in a far higher degree than ordinary Christians who are not bound by the evangelical counsels. Again, while, the object and extent of our vow is exactly determined for all of us by the very definition of the vow itself—so that we may easily recognize and weigh up its importance and gravity—on the other hand, the extent and practice of virtue and the gravity of its obligation are determined by our vocation and the providential circumstances of our lives.

In certain cases it will be evident that we are bound to perform one or perhaps several acts of virtue; and the obligation is all the more imperative when the vow is imperiled and when the vow can only be safeguarded by more diligent practice of virtue.

Anyhow, the fact remains that the essential end of the religious life is to tend to the perfection of charity, and that implies in religious men and women the most perfect possible practice of virtue.

Therefore, self-examination should mean not only inquiring into our manner of keeping our vows, but also testing and proving how we have practiced the virtues: and we are bound to accuse ourselves on this point in Confession. Some may object that there is no formal and serious obligation to do this; but the very *end* of our vocation is perfection in virtue, and the obligation of examining and accusing ourselves on this point is as serious and important in God's eyes as our very vocation itself.

Again, you may admit a certain amount of human perplexity and you may object that the exact manner of practicing this or that virtue, on a given occasion, is neither certain nor clear. This puzzled state of mind arises in great measure precisely from the fact that we confine our examination almost exclusively to our observance of the vows and are not sufficiently concerned about the positive practice of virtue. If we were more deeply penetrated with the consciousness of our exceptional vocation, which is, as it were, a foretaste of our heavenly heritage, a happy fore-shadowing of our eternal destiny; if we had learnt by experience that a religious who does not tend to perfection, sinks below the most miserable mediocrity, we should see much more clearly the purpose of our vocation and the progress in virtue—the growing towards God—which it demands of us; we should recognize and seize more readily the helps and opportunities so lavishly bestowed by God. If we were only enlightened in this matter we should seek out a wise guide and friend, who would lead us in the right way and show us our crying need, namely, that charity should reign in our hearts: charity can only so reign when we dedicate our lives to perfection and when we begin to hunger and thirst after righteousness. We should take heed, lest by our indifference, our lukewarmness, our lack of effort, and our half-heartedness we sink to the level of those who compromise even their solemn obligations and drop out of the fight altogether.

This very thorough carefulness in accusing ourselves in Confession accomplishes not only the work of the purgative way but also initiates us into the illuminative way.

A common complaint among people in the world who go frequently to Confession is that they have very little to accuse themselves of. The habitual insignificance of their trivial faults makes them find within their souls very little room for improvement. What a contrast is presented to the person who looks at his life as a striving after perfection! He sees, rolled out before his eyes, an unending road of infinite possibilities, reaching out to eternity and God. Visible effects will follow from the Sacrament of Penance if we use it with our mind's eye on the main purpose and end of our vocation. Among these visible signs two in particular will appear as the precious fruits of contrition, sanctified by sacramental grace; a certain fusion, or thawing, so to speak, of the stubborn will into a general disposition of humility, and a real contempt of all earthly ties.

Contrition means not only the bruising of the heart by sorrow, but also the breaking of the resistance of the will by obedience. The voice of God more easily reaches souls softened by sorrow or humbled by affliction: so, too, those deaf to God's call will be found to suffer not only from hardness of hearing, but also from hardness of heart. Even gentle and pliable natures will sometimes in their spiritual life reveal unsuspected depths of hardness and obstinacy. God's chosen people, the Israelites, were often upbraided for being a stiff-necked race. In some way we all fall under this reproach: very often pain and suffering are the only means of leading some souls to humility and docility. Whatever means God may choose to work His own good work in us, conversion and spiritual growth are impossible until the rebel self has been brayed and crushed: the will must be ground to powder by contrition so that God may make it anew by His grace.

For us, with our long theological training, formal and deliberate pride ought not to be an easy sin to commit, if indeed it be possible at all. Still, spiritual pride is extremely subtle. Prudence and respectability, when they come into conflict with the interior impulses of grace, easily turn into pride; but of all forms of pride, the most terrifying is the refusal to aspire after progress in the supernatural life. Where shall we find better opportunities for breaking our obstinate wills, for crushing our pride and softening our hard hearts, than when we go to Confession; prostrating ourselves, crying out for pardon and imploring the outpouring of the Precious Blood on our souls?

Sin, we have said, is the turning away from God and a turning towards finite good. Contrition, then, must mean turning back once more to God and disentangling ourselves from all earthly ties. This is the aim of our vow of poverty, to disembarrass us and enable us to turn freely to God. All the scheme of our life of mortification and our penitential observances, apart from their expiating effects, tend to raise us above all the seductions of earthly things. Our frequent confessions should imply frequent reminders of our obligations regarding poverty and mortification and each confession should be an occasion for solemnly renewing our zeal for these two virtues which sacramental grace magnifies and makes sublime. It is through poverty and mortification that we share in the passion of Christ, whose merits the Sacrament applies.

Without humility, poverty, and mortification there is no possible hope of the least degree of experience in the unitive life. These signs of efficacious contrition, humility, and detachment are not weak emotions, but great forces which win for us a serene and joyous mastery and a worthy scorn of all the things of this world.

In her *Dialogue*, St. Catherine, when speaking of the terrible truths about the divine justice, says: "A false Christian shall be more severely punished than a pagan" (Treatise on Discretion). If we go to Confession with the dispositions such as I have described we shall come forth, not false but true Dominicans, and we shall thus forestall the action of the divine justice and rob the last judgment of all its terrors.

XII

The Dominican Doctrine on Grace

I ought perhaps to explain why I call the doctrine of grace our doctrine, since in its leading principles it comes from St. Paul and belongs to the Church. But besides its having been formulated with iron precision by St. Thomas and his school (after St. Augustine), it is superfluous to note that some of its conclusions—and to my mind those most closely connected with the principles—are considered as having been asserted and defended chiefly by us.

I remember, once, when paying a visit with my Novitiate Community to the house of another Order, we found ourselves the object of an inquisitive and almost anxious scrutiny. Our hosts sought to detect the effects of our theological studies on our spiritual life, and they evidently expected to find in us the rigid and hopeless consequences of Calvinism and Jansenism. They were agreeably disappointed to see that the result in our private and common life was just the reverse. It is on no such quest that I embark when I declare my intention of speaking to you of the practical use and application of our doctrine on grace. Its usefulness will be proved by further consideration of the subject. Divine grace may be regarded, firstly, as the primordial vocation of man to the supernatural order; secondly, as a gift habitually dwelling in the justified soul; thirdly, as an actual and indispensable help from above. You will understand I can only skim over so vast and deep a subject.

The practical importance of the doctrine of the primordial vocation of mankind to the supernatural order is unlimited. In it we shall find unending motives for admiration and adoration. It is said of St. Augustine that after his conversion he could never fully satisfy his desire to contemplate the divine plan for the salvation of the human race—that is to say, the idea of the Incarnation; and yet, in truth, the Incarnation is, as far as we can judge of such a mystery, only the remedy to the check which the fall of man gave to an antecedent plan. Let us go back further than the Gospel and put ourselves face to face with that incomprehensible love of God for His creature, which destined us from all eternity to the participation of His essential and infinite Beatitude: for that is exactly what we mean by our vocation to the supernatural order. "*We shall be like unto Him, and see Him as He is, face to face.*" Yes, it is indeed a great mystery, since, as St. Thomas teaches, God loves nothing in us that He has not first caused in us. In the natural order, His providence inclines Him towards the needs of that degree of being that He, as Creator, has imparted to us. In the supernatural order His loving charity inclines Him towards the requirements of our previous vocation to the supernatural Life. *Voluntas hominis movetur ex bono praeexistente in rebus;…bonum creaturae provenit ex voluntate divina*—"The will of man is moved by the good pre-existing in things… for the good of a creature springs from the Divine will" (*Summa Theologiae*, I–II.110, a. 1).

The love of God is ever gratuitous, and, for that very reason, ever incomprehensible. To this principle we have to refer all the mysteries of Faith, in their attractive as well as their terrifying aspects—I do not say in order to explain them, but even to be able to hold to their adorable complexity of light and shadow. The mystery of individual predestination, for instance, which includes prospects both astonishingly touching and terrible, is said to be a consequence of the supreme independence of the First Cause. What does this mean but the absolute gratuitousness of the Love of God? When referred to this principle, the darkness of the mysteries of faith is simply adorable; it makes us lose ourselves in the incomprehensible goodness of God:

> O how far removed, predestination! is thy root from such as see not the First Cause entire! (*Paradiso*, XX:130)

> Such scantiness of knowledge our delight: For all our good is, in that primal good, Concentrate; and God's will and ours are one. (*Paradiso*, XX:136)

This great doctrine of the elevation of mankind to the supernatural order should be a frequent subject of our meditation; it should never be shunned as a danger.

The practical utility of this doctrine is shown also in the fact that it is hardly possible to understand the literal meaning of many texts of the Gospel, and certainly impossible to enter into their inner meaning, unless the distinction between the natural and supernatural is kept well in view. When Our Lord tells us that to know Him is Life Eternal, that no one cometh to the Father but by Him, and none to Him unless drawn by the Father; when He exacts from His followers such great renunciations; when

He curses the spirit of the world; when He unceasingly speaks of Light, and yet without casting the faintest light on natural science; when He promises happiness at the cost of persecution and sacrifice; finally, when we see that, since His time, the Church and the influence of the Gospel have done so little to change the natural order of things, then we begin to grasp the meaning of a Supreme Life, which is not only an addition to the present life, but absolutely transcends it, as it transcends all our human hopes and aspirations. If we deprive all these ideas of the light cast on them by the notion of the supernatural, they lose their force, and almost cease to be in accordance with the initial mystery of the Incarnation. Unless the supernatural rule of interpretation is admitted, the writings of St. Paul are those of a madman.

Moreover, the notion of the supernatural order is indispensable, if we would attempt to understand that violation of order implied in the fall of the angels, to a due appreciation of the mysterious disorder of creation itself "which groaneth and travaileth, until the time of its redemption"; and finally to a due appreciation of the disorder of our own nature, so deeply divided against itself. Nor can we realize our true position before God without some comparative notion of the different states, real or possible, of mankind: the state of pure nature, the state of original justice, the state of fallen nature, the state of redeemed nature—which all refer to the fundamental concept of the supernatural order.

The revelation of our vocation to participate in Eternal Life constitutes the most striking characteristic of the Gospel, and its unparalleled greatness. This doctrine is in itself an apologia. It is the purest of all the glories of the Church. It is the finest of the jewels with which the cappa of St. Thomas was seen studded: "*Ex monili fulgoris caelici, lux emissa mundo diffunditur*" (Liturgy of the Hours, Office of St. Thomas Aquinas).[†] I think this is one of the main objects of our teaching and preaching office, one of the main forces of our apostolate. Its power on all men, learned and unlearned, is inexhaustible—when the teacher is fully convinced of its reality, of its beauty, of its importance. It is a joy to remember how Père Lacordaire penetrated the supernatural idea at a time when the supernatural aspect of Christianity was very little recognized. Hence came many blessings on his labors, and I believe that to this he owed his glorious mission as restorer of the Order.

Here, again, you see in a new light the practical usefulness of our doctrine.

On the other, hand, nothing is safe when grace is confounded with nature. Such confusion results in the negation of grace itself. It is significant that the confused system, which in the present day goes under the name of "immanence," coincides with an error which reduces the Sacraments to the level of mere practical rites, and denies their reality. Reverence and gratitude to God cease when the notion of our supernatural destiny grows feeble and dim.

The doctrine of divine grace, since it implies a supernatural gift abiding in the justified soul, must have a real practical command over our lives. We should strive to understand what is meant by *sanctifying grace*. It must not be identified with the theological or moral virtues; it is something more, it is a quality by which God imbues the very essence of the soul with something of His own nature. That deep source of our manifold activity is mingled with a divine energy, so that the faculties derived from it ought to produce acts fused into a divine alloy. For this reason it is said that sanctifying grace is in us *as a nature—per modum*

[†]   "From the collar of heavenly brightness, a light is poured forth sent out to the world."

naturae—that is, as an inherent and personal principle of action.

Beautifully does St. Thomas express this, when he says that God has to provide His creatures not less in the supernatural than in the natural order, with informing principles of action, so that the creatures may be moved of their own impulse, and not only by occasional fits and starts (see *Summa Theologiae*, I–II.110, a. 2).

Sanctifying grace, being somewhat of a sharing in the Divine Nature, draws with it a special and loving presence in us of the Divine Persons. I am sorry I can but allude, in passing, to this greatest of all wonders worked in the soul by sanctifying grace. To expound the mystical indwelling of the soul by the Divine Persons would require a long treatise. I will only point out the practical results of a doctrine that reveals to us a fact so utterly beyond our ordinary experience. The ascetical rule of *Recollection* is inspired by, and founded on, the sanctifying presence of the Blessed Trinity in us. Recollection, with us, is no unnatural tension of our powers towards an abstract object, not a violent effort of internal realization, but simply the consciousness of the loving presence of God in us, which initiates the possession of those realities to be hoped for. It is the actual and living belief in the words of Our Lord: "If any one love Me, he will keep My word, and My Father will love him, and We will come to him, and will make Our abode with him" (John 24:23.) It is impossible to be convinced of the truth of these words without, at the same time, crying out to God: *Averte oculos meos ne videant vanitatem* (Psalm 119:37—"Turn my eyes from what is false."), which is the very voice of the soul turning from created things to seek the living God within.

The presence of the Divine Persons endows us with the gift of "Unction"—a keen and persuasive instinct, which keeps us on the trail of divine grace. It is through spiritual unction that, as St. Thomas teaches, "those who need to be led by the advice of others, know nevertheless how to direct themselves, *if they have grace in themselves*, because they do not shrink from seeking counsel, and they discern the good from the bad" (*Summa Theologiae*, II–II.47, a. 14).

Observe the wonderful autonomy of the Christian soul. Observe the dignity and liberty that divine grace preserves in it, in the very moment that it bows to obedience.

If, generally speaking, habit is a second nature, how much more is that divine quality engrafted in our very spiritual substance, which we term sanctifying grace!

Consequently, the first thing to observe is that, by being justified, we are utterly and completely renewed. The natural order becomes inadequate to our powers, and we have incessantly to emerge from it. Grace, in this sense, is a sort of creation, according to the fine words of St. Thomas: "Grace is said to be created, from the fact that men are created anew by it; they are made out of nothing, and without their own merits, into new beings."

The practical question with us is to prove to ourselves that we have, as a result of this new birth, also new instincts and inclinations. Such are called by St. Paul the "*mind of Christ*" and, in ordinary language, the supernatural spirit. Remember that you can no longer content yourselves with acting from natural motives. That you ought to accomplish in a new and more perfect manner even indifferent actions and common duties. You must, without ceasing to be men, cease to be human. Woe to you if you no longer feel in the depths of your hearts the throbbings of supernatural instincts! Worse still, if you fear to be different from men of the world. It would be a proof that, instead of the living waters springing up unto life everlasting, you contain only stagnant pools, from which even the world would turn away in disgust.

Behold on what real foundations the supernatural spirit is based. Another thing to be observed is that grace, being rooted in the very substance of our soul, manifests itself not in deceptive emotions of passing devotion and enthusiasm, but in the acts of the noblest faculties of our justified and sanctified souls: reason enlightened by Faith, and will aided by Grace. These are the true organs of the divine life in us; and such acts are the genuine product of our regenerated nature.

It may seem superfluous to insist on the necessity of acting from reason enlightened by Faith and from will aided by Grace; yet there are few whose inner life proceeds habitually from the depths of their souls. There are many, on the contrary, who not only neglect and ignore the supernatural powers which come from abiding grace and which strengthen with new energy our natural faculties, but who seem also to ignore and neglect even those chief organs of rational life, intelligence and will. We cannot consider acts proceeding from feeling and imagination, fruitful of substantial results. You often hear, nowadays, from certain dabblers in theology that we must go to God with our whole soul; which saying, under cover of openmindedness, minimizes the part that the intellect has to play in our adherence to God. Ethical sensitiveness is regarded, nowadays, as the best conductor of divine light. Let us note that going to God with one's whole soul firstly and mainly implies an act of intelligence and will; all the so-called intuitions of the heart are not worth one good act of reason and will. Here you have an exact illustration of the result of confused notions of supernatural principles. It is all too true that we are tending to a Christianity made up of sentiment; devotion is taking the place of faith and virtue, not to say of duty, whereas it should be its outcome.

Let us persuade ourselves that it matters very little, after all, if the spiritual life is interesting or not, if prayer is sweet or arid, if virtue is easy or difficult. The one thing necessary is that all our activity should come from our very soul, and return to it. All true virtue originates from reason and will. In the Christian soul the virtues are, in fact, the royal escort of sanctifying grace; they have no longer to do with the senses, except that they exact from them service, and they reward that service with the overflow of their own joy.

Look at the high standard of conduct that is involved in the doctrine of sanctifying grace. We are children no longer: with St. Paul, we must "put away the things of a child" and be conscious of manhood renewed in Christ.

As to the third aspect of the doctrine of grace, we believe not only that divine grace is necessary for all the acts of our Christian life, but also that those very acts, in what in them is most personal and free, receive from God, the *agens principale*, all their formal perfections: *Non solum autem a Deo est omnis motio, sicut a primo movente, sed etiam ab ipso est omnis formalis perfectio, sicut a Primo Actu* (*Summa Theologiae*, I–II.109, a. 1). This implies that no good really belongs to us. Yet, *free* we remain; and prayer, though it cannot be made without grace, does not lack the power of obtaining it. This implies that our spiritual life is based not only on fidelity to grace, but on the deep consciousness and the indisputable conviction of our absolute dependence on divine grace. This goes further than the simple belief in the necessity of supernatural charity to make our works meritorious; it goes further than belief in a concourse of the divine and human activity; even further than belief in the Sacred Humanity of Our Lord as the meritorious and instrumental cause of all graces. The Dominican doctrine of the continual need and the absolute efficacy of grace confront us with the all-embracing and all-efficient causality of God; it shows the divine causality claiming for itself all action of ours achieved in the supernatural order; as, in the natural order, the divine motion claims for itself all the exercise of our activity. Such a statement does not lead to fatalism, nor to quietism: this is an intelligent and noble doctrine, which refrains from the attempt to explain the liberty of man by limiting the liberty and the power of God, which is fully conscious of the difficulties that may arise from its principles, but holds nevertheless that principles ought not to be sacrificed to objections, strong though the latter may be. This is the doctrine of men such as St. Paul, St. Augustine, St. Thomas, Bossuet, who were by no means fakirs or idlers. On the contrary, these men felt that never were they so much masters of themselves, and never did they use their energy so generously, as when they gave to God the homage of all their human activity. Moreover, what do we do, when we try to bring souls to God, to conform them to the spirit of the Gospel, what, but convince them of their own nothingness, and that without God they can do no good thing? Do we not begin by teaching them that all that belongs to them is deficiency and sin, and that they absolutely depend on prayer and help from above? Until we have led these souls to say to God, in sincerity and truth: "As the eyes of the servant are on her mistress, so have we waited on the Lord until He has pity upon us" (Psalm 123:2), we hardly believe that they have taken the first step in the spiritual life. What is this but to enter practically into the doctrine of all-efficient grace?

Not only does this doctrine imply the preparatory virtues of humility, self-distrust, and obedience, but also it guides us towards the end of the spiritual life, which is perfection, wisdom, and union with God. The most precious fruit of experience that ripens in us as the years go by is the conviction that it was not we who directed our steps on the path of life, but God who worked everything in us of His own good pleasure; and that we, by our self-will and self-agitation, marred the divine work. Let us then rest in the hands of God, depend entirely on His grace, and let us be grateful for our strong training in the doctrine of grace, which we have received in the Order. If we, with St. Catherine, recognize in our Order a spirit, magnanimous, large, and free, let us conclude that God thus rewards in us the gift of loyalty and fidelity to divine grace, which He has Himself bestowed upon us.

XIII

Dominican Devotion to Our Lord

There is in the tenth chapter of St. John's Gospel a wonderful scene, in which Our Lord appears, so to say, as the Divine Peripatetic, not only in His exterior attitude, but also in His way of arguing with the Jews. He walked in the temple in Solomon's Porch: there He taught some of His supreme lessons, both as to His Divinity and His Humanity. Apart from the striking vividness and picturesque glory of this passage and the beauty of the vision that it unexpectedly opens before us—since Our Lord there appears much in the same guise, yet superior to the greatest masters of Greek wisdom—I wish only to link up with this scene and the words in the Gospel the two principal characteristics of Dominican devotion to Our Lord.

As I have already said, we, as champions of the Faith, have for the Faith a chivalrous devotion; but, we may ask, Does this special character of chivalry stand out when it is a question of devotion to Our Lord? From the preeminently doctrinal vocation of the Order and also from the history of our mystics it would seem that our devotion to Christ bears something of an abstract character; it leads us to linger, though not indeed exclusively, on that which is highest in the mystery of the Incarnation, I mean on the divine nature and Person of Our Lord. You remember how Blessed Henry Suso, who of all our mystics seems to be tinged with romanticism, was accustomed to consider Our Lord as the type of the Eternal Wisdom. But the testimony of St. Thomas is still more significant and suggestive:

> Those things which belong to the Divinity are, *in themselves*, the strongest incentive to love and consequently to devotion...Yet such is the weakness of the human mind that it needs a guiding hand not only to lead it to the knowledge of God, but also to the love of Divine things by means of certain sensible objects already known to us... Chief among these is the humanity of Christ...

> Wherefore matters relating to Christ's humanity are the chief incentive to devotion, leading us as by a guiding hand, although devotion itself has for its object the things which concern the Godhead: *cum tamen devotio principaliter circa ea quae sunt divinitatis consistat.* (*Summa Theologiae*, II–II.82, a. 3)

This explains what I mean when I say our devotion to Our Lord is rather abstract than chivalrous, or if you prefer, chivalrous in a more ideal sense.

The lesson of Solomon's Porch should come home to us in a very special way: we as disciples in the school of Jesus Christ, the greatest of Masters, should always by word and work echo His teaching with enthusiastic devotion. All our mysticism and, above all, St. Thomas's treatise on the Incarnation, are but a commentary on these words of Christ: "My Father is greater than all"; "My Father and I are one." And just as Our Lord mingles with this sublime teaching simple images of the pastoral life: "My sheep hear My voice; I know them, and they will follow Me, and I will give to them Life Eternal"; so also we must see in Dominican life a pasture in which the highest objects of Faith become food and life to the soul.

Our devotion, then, to Our Lord is devotion to the God-Christ, devotion to the Eternal Truth, to the Divine Word, living in and personally united with the Sacred Humanity of Jesus.

Innumerable will be the effects on our lives of such devotion. The very least we can say is that it keeps us from lowering and weakening in our souls the idea (and, in our worship and ministry, the image) of Our Lord Jesus Christ. It is impossible to ignore the sad fact that such a lowering tendency is manifest everywhere as a general tedency of the present day; it has resulted in widespread irreverence, and, on the part of many believers, in a deplorable indifference and inconsistency. It is truly an alarming symptom! Where is our robust Christianity? Where are our vigorous, wholehearted Christians today? It is easy to be irritated by this unhealthy tendency in its more obvious material manifestations, when for example we meet with debased religious art and certain mawkish and empty forms of prayer. But there is very little difference between such cheapness and vulgarity and the childish aggressiveness of subjective criticism against theology.

To us Our Lord appears, above all else, as the *Geminae Gigas Substantiae* ("a giant in twofold substance one"). Yes, a Giant, and, even in His Humanity, terrible, mighty, majestic. The Faith of the Middle Ages was not barbaric or rude, when it preferred to consider Our Lord as the Judge of all men; when it took delight in placing Him over the arches of the sanctuaries in the center of terrifying Apocalyptic scenes; when it depicted Him of gigantic

size in the apses, as if to fill the whole church with His Presence;
and when it gave even to the figures of His Childhood powerful
proportions to express the greatness of the Divine Mind.

It might be said that, within the Church, many people seem
to put a weak element into their devotion to Christ, not indeed
anything opposed to theological tenets, but something of a senti-
mentally sympathetic and protective nature. The development,
otherwise remarkable, of the idea of reparation towards Our
Lord seems to be understood by some as their solicitude for one
distressed and hopeless. And even chivalrous worship contains
something of a sentiment of pity for the weakness and destitution
of the object of its devotion. Our devotion to Our Lord leads
us further than these considerations. We in no way repudiate
our simple duty of advancing on earth Christ's accidental glory,
but, first and before all, we rejoice and glory in His Essential and
Eternal glory, which is immutable and inalienable. We do not
lose sight of the crown of thorns, but we strive to see shining on
His brow the diadem of the Divine Attributes. "Christ dies now
no more," says St. Paul. He is not only beyond the reach of the
blows of His enemies (even on the Cross the Divine Person drank
bliss at its Source in the Beatific Life of the Three-in One); but
also His great work as our Redeemer, if apparently doomed to
fail, must ultimately be crowned with the triumph of His Divine
Attributes. Truly, no devotion to Our Lord, no zeal for His glory
on earth could be worthy of Him, if irreconcilable with, and
estranged from, a living joy in His Divine and Eternal Glory.
Our Lord's only prayer for Himself had no concern for His own
accidental glory on earth, but, as it seems, the full splendor of
the Eternal Glory of His risen Humanity. "Glorify Thou Me, O
Father, *with Thyself—apud temetipsum—*with the Glory that I had
before the world was, with Thee" (John 17:5.) We may reserve
our protecting compassion for men on earth; it is our duty to

work till death, if need be, for the interests and salvation of their souls, but, for pity's sake, let us talk less about the interests of Our Lord. Let us pay to His eternal glory and beatitude the homage of our joy, which is the true mark of supernatural love. Let us preach, and spread abroad the *greatest* glory of Our Divine Lord. I have sufficiently pointed out that it will not exclude rejoicing in His Cross. *Ad Maximam Jesu Christi Gloriam!*

In the tenth chapter of St. John, with which we began our instruction, the Divine Peripatetic says that His sheep hear His voice, and He knows them, and they follow Him, and that no man shall pluck them out of His hand, because that which His Father hath given Him is greater than all, and no one can snatch them out of the hand of His Father. Then, as the Jews take stones to stone Him, in arguing with them, He uses an argument *a fortiori* to prove that He is the Son of God. As a base of His argument He admits a certain participating deification of man, expressed in the Old Testament and to be realized even more fully in the Christian soul by His own grace.

There we have a clear assertion of the everlasting power of the Sacred Humanity as the instrumental cause of grace for the justification, sanctification, and salvation of all souls. To this again we can very appropriately refer the second characteristic of Dominican devotion to Our Lord, namely faith in the invisible, universal, and unceasing influence of the Sacred Humanity as the channel of Divine Grace. Clearly, then, we do not allow ourselves to be absorbed in a mere ideal and abstract devotion to Our Lord. We turn frequently to His adorable Humanity to derive force and strength from that mysterious and continuous intercession exercised by Him in heaven: "He ever liveth to make intercession for us." But intercession conveys too little: in a close and intimate sense we have to be welded into His own

Divine Life so as to reproduce in us that Sacred Humanity itself, and thus extend the life of His mystical Body even here on earth.

The motto of our devotion to the Sacred Humanity might well be: "*He has ascended into heaven to fill all things*" (see Eph. 4:10). Attraction, gravitation, and all the forces that reach this little planet are not more real than the divine energy which, through the sacred wounds of Our Lord, incessantly works upon us. St. Catherine, as you remember, compares the Sacred Humanity to a bridge, which unites heaven and earth, and is the only means of passing from one to the other; but how can we draw near to this Sacred Humanity since it is so far above us, and since the Holy Eucharist provides only a passing union with it? Here the symbol used by St. Catherine needs completion: the Divinity itself of Our Lord may in its turn be symbolized as a bridge between the Son of Man and the sons of men. The Sacred Humanity can fill the world with its sanctifying influences only in virtue of the Infinite Power, from which it is inseparable. Thus Our Lord, glorified in heaven, is for us both the type we have to imitate and the working-power that elaborates its likeness in us. Thus, "He is not far from each one of us, and in Him we live, and move, and have our being" (Acts 17:28). Thus, it is not only His evangelical life, which is the model of our own lives, but still more the present dispositions of His Blessed Soul in heaven.

The prayer attributed to St. Thomas, which is perhaps more ancient than his time, *Anima Christi sanctissima, sanctifica me*, is not an empty figure. Thus are fulfilled the words of the Divine Master Himself in our text: "I give them life everlasting…and no man shall pluck them out of My hand. That which My Father hath given Me is greater than all"—(or, from another version, "My Father is greater than all")—"and no man can snatch them out of the hand of My Father" (John 10:29). Thus, finally, our deification by sanctifying grace, and every increase of that inner gift, as well as every actual grace all the days of our life, is due to the Sacred Humanity. Therefore the Man-Christ confronts us step by step with, and brings us to, the God-Christ. The Divine Essence is the adequate object of eternal life which Christ's Humanity merits for us, and which His grace begins in us. Let us aspire, with St. Augustine, to that life to come, when we will see not only the Son of Mary full of grace and truth, but see also the Son of the Eternal Father face to face, and hear the Divine Word without the sound of human speech:

Qualis erit vita de Verbo sine Verbo? Modo ista vivebat de Verbo, sed sonante verbo. Erit vita de Verbo, nullo sonante verbo. Ipsum Verbum vita est. (St. Augustine, Sermon 169)

XIV

Adoro Te Devote

The *Adoro Te* of St. Thomas Aquinas is the highest and best expression of all we can say in a brief space about the Blessed Sacrament. Let me make two preliminary remarks.

In the first place, we should find it impossible to think of the Blessed Sacrament without deep gratitude to God for having allowed our Order the privilege of doing such great things—if we may so dare to speak—for the Church's official worship of this glorious Sacrament. St. Thomas is the Theologian, and the sacred Songster of the Eucharist. Not only has he given perfect utterance to the formulae of the faith in this Sacrament, but he has also left to the Church the most perfect forms of praise and prayer; so that we can hardly enter a church, either in town or country, without hearing, and without there rising to our lips, words which are the echo of his own love and devotion. It must fill our hearts with true and joyful emotion to see our Order bound by such special ties to the greatest of the Sacraments, and to find forever associated with the Eucharistic doctrine and worship the teaching of our glorious Doctor and the genius of the Order itself. "He hath not done so in any other nation" (Psalm 147:20). Secondly, from the very words of the hymn on which we are about to meditate, we may infer that private devotion to the Blessed Sacrament—that is to say, devotion to the Real Presence quite apart from the Sacrifice and Holy Communion—must appeal to us in a special way. Not only does the *Adoro Te* seem to be a prayer for private use, to be said before the tabernacle at all hours of the day, but also, even in the hymns of the liturgical office composed by St. Thomas, a personal note rings out most touchingly.

> *Dedit   et   tristibus   sanguinis   poculum...*
> *...Nova   sint   omnia*
> *Corda, voces, et opera...*

> On   them,   downcast   and   sad,
> His   Blood   bestowed   He...
> ...   and   all   be   new   around,
> in every act, and voice, and heart.

Such expressions surely spring from the deepest feelings of the individual soul; in a direct and forcible manner they concern our personal lives rather than the collective life of the Church. They breathe the most intimate aspirations of the spiritual life; they are filled with the consciousness of our human misery, of our personal effort against sin, and of our striving after perfection. The prayer included in the form of thanksgiving after Mass reads like a commentary on these Eucharistic hymns of St. Thomas, in so far as they are available for private devotion and expressive of it.

In a remarkable study on *The Christian Altar*, the learned liturgist Mr. Edmund Bishop illustrates the preeminence of the great Sacrifice in the public worship in the churches of the Mid-

dle Ages. From the documents which he quotes it would seem
that, generally speaking, the reservation of the Blessed Sacrament, though of course acknowledged by tokens of real adoration, was mainly intended for the use of the sick. Thus we know
but little about private devotion to the real Presence apart from
the time of Mass and of Communion. It seems to me that the
prayers of St. Thomas throw light on the question of private
devotion to the Blessed Sacrament as practiced before our own
time, and we may see in the *Adoro Te* the first and best form of
prayer for "*visits to the Blessed Sacrament*."

> *Adoro   Te   devote,   latens   Deitas,*
> *Quae   sub   his   figuris   vere   latitas;*
> *Tibi   se   cor   meum   totum   subjicit,*
> *Quia Te contemplans totum deficit.*

> Devoutly   I   adore   Thee,   Godhead   unrevealed,
> In below this shape and show present, close concealed;
> Lowly   I   make   obeisance;   all   the   wits   in   me
> Faint and fail me wholly contemplating Thee.[†]

This may be termed the verse of overpowering adoration. The
Presence that fills our churches is not only a Real Presence, but
also a sensible Presence. It is not on that feeling that our faith is
based, yet, varying as it may be in its manifestations and intensity,
the fact of this experience is not a thing to be neglected or ignored,
since nearly all the faithful, and very often unbelievers too, bear
witness to its existence. Christ is to us, as He was to the disciples at
Emmaus, the companion of our journey, and when He hides His
face, or when the hearts of men are *hard and slow to believe*, His

---

[†]   Original note: We have given throughout J. S. Phillimore's metrical translation.

Divine Presence radiates within us, either to warn or rebuke us, if we are unworthy to stand before Him or approach Him. *Adoro Te* is not a cry that rises from our hearts when we enter a church where there is no tabernacle, but it comes spontaneously to our lips as we fall on our knees on entering the threshold of one of our own churches. What a contrast between this feeling which casts us on our knees, and the insignificant appearance of the Sacramental Elements! That kind of conflict between our faith and our imagination with regard to the Divine Presence might be expected if we came before It enthroned with pomp and visible glory: but the Real Presence is the silent continuation of the Sacrifice, the Victim reduced to the humblest attitude and to almost contemptible proportions—motionless and, so to say, annihilated. And yet we feel Its presence and Its power.

Adoro Te devote, latens Deitas —"Devoutly I adore Thee, Godhead unrevealed"; let us say it in church, let us say it out of church; let us repeat it when from afar we see the spire of the church where He is present. When the beauties of nature enthrall our gaze, when mountain and vale lay spread before us, when our hearts take upward flight to the Creator, then let us remember the Eucharistic Presence on earth of the Incarnate God. Let us, with an all-embracing eye, survey the places where He multiplies the Presence of His humanity.

Still more, when before the tabernacle, let us enter into that darkness of faith and into the sacred silence of the Eucharistic mystery. Because it is an overpowering mystery, our act of adoration is inexhaustible. The little door of the tabernacle opens into the Infinite, and the life which pulsates in the Host is that of the Heart of Jesus Christ.

Visus,	*gustus,*	*tactus*	*in*	*Te*	*fallitur,*
Sed	*auditu*	*solo*	*tuto*		*creditur.*

Credo quidquid dixit Dei Filius:
Nil hoc veritatis Verbo verius.

Vision, touch and taste are all outwitted here,
Yet I trust my hearing, sure of that I hear:
Spoken by the Son of God every word is sooth:
Nothing can be truer than the Word of Truth.

The second verse brings before us the sacramental miracle
in virtue of which the signs or elements of the Holy Eucharist
are devoid of their substance, while the Humanity of Christ is
substantially present without sensible appearance. There are in
this Sacrament many other miracles, but all are derived from
that wondrous conversion of substance. Faith alone can give us
an idea of the possibility of such a distinction in the constitutive
elements of things. Faith alone shows us God penetrating into
the depths of created things and, by the sword of the sacramental
word, dividing substance from accidents. So here it is not the
miracle that has to play the part of confirming the faith, but it
is faith that has to guarantee the Eucharistic miracle. An explicit
act of faith must immediately follow the act of adoration.

The Eucharistic miracle has a wide bearing in the theological
field, nay even in the domain of philosophy, since almost all the
difficulties of philosophers, nowadays, converge upon the question of substance. That, once admitted and believed, clinches
our faith, and makes it as tempered steel. The Blessed Sacrament
is the compendium of all the dogmas, as well as the principle of
all the sacraments and the source of all moral perfection.

Just because the Holy Eucharist claims the soul's very highest faith, because it is the Incarnation continued and renewed
in all ages, because it is the foundation of the Church and the
pledge of eternal life, therefore the Blessed Sacrament in a sense

makes faith easier. Let us then lead to the Holy Eucharist souls that seek faith, and those who seek its increase. Our apostolate should be inspired by the Divine Oracle from the Altar. Pointing to the Sacred Host, we should say to all men: "*Didst thou but know the gift of God?*"

The two following verses:

In cruce latebat sola Deitas…

and:

Plagas, sicut Thomas, non intueor…

On the cross tho' God was hid, Man was plain to view;
Here the very manhood disappeareth too:
Yet I do believe thee both, both I do avow:
As the thief in penitence I beseech thee now.

Thomas saw Thy woundprints: seeing, he adored.
I that cannot see them hail Thee God and Lord.
Let it be that faith in Thee grows without surcease;
Hope and Love together more and more increase.

take us back to the Passion of Our Lord. In them we have a petition for the three chief benefits which are the proper effects of the Holy Eucharist; first, the application of the Redemption to each of us in particular, that is to say the renewal of pardon and its extension to all our daily sins. Then a petition that the Blessed Sacrament may be to us a pledge of life eternal: both are contained in those touching words:

Peto quod petivit latro poenitens.

I make the selfsame prayer as the repentant thief.

The good thief was the first of the redeemed: he asked and obtained a promise of salvation. In the same way we hope that the Holy Eucharist, either as a sacrifice or through Holy Communion, will be to us a daily renewal of redemption: in return for the memory of Our Lord which we keep in the Holy Eucharist, He will remember us in His Kingdom. The third benefit that flows from the Blessed Sacrament is the increase of the supernatural life in us, by the growth of Faith, Hope, and Charity. These are the mainsprings of the redeemed soul: they command all other virtues. Therefore, St. Thomas says:

> *Fac   me   tibi   semper   magis   credere,*
> *In Te spem habere, te diligere.*

> Let it be that Faith in Thee grow without surcease.
> Hope and Love together more and more increase.

St. Thomas continues by imploring two secondary effects of sacramental grace, namely the spiritual enjoyment of the divine Bread, and purity of heart.

> *Praesta   meae   menti   de   te   vivere,*
> *Et   te   illi   semper   dulce   sapere...*
> *...Me immundum munda tuo Sanguine.*

> Always make my soul to take Thee for livelihood,
> Always grant that I may taste and find it good...
> ...Jesus, in Thy cleansing blood be my sins forgiven.

Such effects are only implicitly contained in the evangelical promise and institution of the Holy Eucharist. It is by the widespread experience of saints, through long ages, that these effects have been attached to Holy Communion. It seems that, in primitive times, men had recourse to Holy Communion rather to gain strength and faith than to seek spiritual sweetness and consolation. The heavenly Bread was for them primarily the indispensable and substantial daily bread. In the strong souls of the martyrs there was little leisure for, and perhaps less seeking after, joy and consolation.

As to purity of heart, its relation to Holy Communion is manifested in history both sooner and more explicitly; as when St. Paul says: "First, let a man prove himself, and then let him eat of this bread" (1 Cor. 11:28), from the beginning it shows itself either as a preparatory condition or as the affinity of virgin souls with the Bread of Angels rather than as a special effect. We all now admit—what we may have actually experienced—the efficacy of Holy Communion for calming the passions and refreshing the heart. We should arouse in ourselves an eager desire for this Heavenly Bread by frequently recalling the death and Passion of Our Lord, which are the price He paid to purchase for us this divine nourishment and saving remedy. Indifference and even distaste for the Bread of Angels is often the punishment of forgetfulness of the Cross of Jesus Christ.

The last verse:

Jesu,	*quem*	*velatum*	*nunc*	*aspicio*
Oro,	*fiat*	*illud*	*quod*	*tam*	*sitio,*
Ut,	*Te*	*revelata*	*cernens*	*facie,*

Visu sim beatus tuae gloriae.

Jesus, whom I darkly thro' these veils discern,
Grant that consummation after which I yearn:
Let mine eyes beholding face to face the Christ
In the glorious vision rest imparadised.

transcends all the temporal effects of the Holy Eucharist. There
is in it a longing for communion with the divine glory of Jesus.
Communion awakens in us desire, which is the response to the
burning desires of Our Lord when He saw in the Last Supper a
prelude of the Eternal Communion with His elect in Heaven:
"With desire I have desired to eat this Pasch with you, before I
suffer, for, I say to you that from this time I will not eat it till it
be fulfilled in the Kingdom of God." (Luke 22:15.) Our contact
with the Sacred Humanity of Jesus gives us such a foretaste of
the all-sufficient Goodness, that we yearn after something else,
something more than Eucharistic Communion. In spite of its
being a wonderful answer to the infinite hunger of the human
heart, the Eucharistic Communion, compared with that which
is eternal, seems almost a figure and a shadow. Needless to warn
you against those devout exaggerations, certainly devoid of the
true Thomistic note, which make of the Eucharist a Sacrament
of Eternity. If in the words "Cleanse me in Thy Blood" ("*me im-
mundum munda Tuo sanguine*") we may catch, perhaps, a far-off
echo of the victorious struggle of St. Thomas against the enemies
of his purity, with much better reason can we hear in this last
verse the homeward longings of his heart, oppressed and wea-
ry with the human quest of things sublime, incomprehensible,
even with the assistance of revealed principles, to the mind of an
angelic mortal such as he was.

There is in the rubrics of our Mass, just before the communion of the priest, a small but most significant rite, which seems
to me to suggest a daily test of fidelity to Our Lord. You know

it well; you know that after having dropped the particle of the divided Host into the Precious Blood to affirm the living unity in Christ, we have to kiss the rim of the chalice. The meaning of this rubric is that the *osculum pacis*, which is to be transmitted through the priest to the faithful, comes from the Divine Priest Himself, and is truly the *osculum Domini*. May we not also see in it a reminder of the Eucharistic ordeal, administered in the Middle Ages to persons from whom an important confession or an urgent justification was demanded? Or more likely still, may not this rite have a more remote meaning, and be linked to the kiss of Judas, or the embrace of St. John? Anyhow, let us take it as a test of our loyalty to Our Lord, a test to be daily renewed. Remember that Our Lord, in the Blessed Sacrament, is the ideal type of the religious. There He is in absolute poverty; there He is in absolute obedience to the priest; there He is freed from all material conditions and laws. Our daily intercourse with Him at the Altar ought to help us to conform more and more to His image and likeness; ought to help us to say more truly every day: "*Voluntarie sacrificabo Tibi*," "I will freely sacrifice unto Thee." (Ps. liii.) So let us never kiss the rim of the chalice, before taking the Precious Blood, without such a renewal of our devotion and the wholehearted ratifying of our profession and the consecration of our whole being:

> *Praesta   meae   menti   de   Te   vivere,*
> *Et Te illi semper dulce sapere.*

> O my Lord's memorial, to bear His death in mind;
> Living Bread, none in Thy stead quickens human kind:
> Always make my soul to take Thee for livelihood,
> Always grant that I may taste and find it good.

XV

Sancta Maria Supra Minervam

O ur Order claims for itself, not only the maternal patronage of the Blessed Virgin, but also the privilege of being the child of her prayers. There is no need here to allude to the testimony of our Chronicles and of our Constitutions; nor need we recall the tradition, expressive and significant as it is, of the giving of the scapular by Our Lady to Blessed Reginald. My present intention is rather to point out how the first manifestations of the specific character of our Order are closely connected with the first tokens of Mary's motherly protection. It is from the time of St. Dominic's first struggles with the heretics that tradition dates the inspiration of the Rosary, originally perhaps a method of preaching rather than a method of prayer. Thus from the very first Most Holy Mary appears as the upholder of Dominic's office of Champion of the Faith; she appears, so to say, as the *Minerva* of the Order. Later, and all through the ages, the Order has never failed to attribute to her its successes and its happy deliverance from its foes; just as the Church herself always flies to the unfailing intercession of Our Lady, confident that she will help in every difficulty and win success for any apostolic enterprise. Therefore, on the day when the

Order was entrusted with a church on the ruins of the temple of Minerva in Rome, Providence itself set its seal on the relationship between our doctrinal mission and the Motherhood of Mary.

From these facts we may gather the special nature of our devotion to the Blessed Virgin, and the ideal type of Mary, which our Order has always specially cherished.

Nothing is more beautiful than the way in which the Church has drawn from the few light touches and scattered references in the Gospel story the perfect image of Mary. The world leaves to theologians the study of those prerogatives which exalt Our Lady as the co-redeemer of mankind and give to her a share in the distribution of graces. All must agree in their admiration of the Catholic type of the Virgin Mother, in whom we recognize the supreme ideal of the superlatively perfect woman; yet with all our marveling love we fall short of complete understanding of her excelling dignity. Still, with all our limitations and without going beyond the simple Gospel narrative, we can find in Mary's character features of stupendous beauty. We should like to show here how the Gospel reveals her as a perfect type of wisdom.

Wisdom is the most excellent of the intellectual virtues. Its object is the consideration of the highest causes and the most sublime aspects of things. It is a certain participation in the infinite and eternal Wisdom. St. Thomas observes that it judges, regulates, and sets in order all the other virtues: for Christians, wisdom is a guiding principle of life, while for the pagan philosophers it was only a speculative power. Now we know that Our Lady was elevated to a special manner of union with the Divine Wisdom: she is the mother and the spouse of the Eternal Wisdom: so the Gospel teaches. Again, if wisdom means the consideration, not only of the deductions and conclusions of science, but, in the first place, of scientific principles (*utitur principiis non solum concludendo, sed judicando de eis*—see *Summa Theologiae*, I–II.66, a. 5, ad. 4), we find in the Gospel Our Lady possessed of all the revealed principles of the Redemption. We see her pondering in her heart the original circumstances of the Incarnation, and on the day of her Purification being given a glimpse of Calvary. On this hint of the Gospel concerning the inner life of Our Lady, Canon Sanday beautifully observes: "'Mary kept all these sayings': *kept* means *continued to keep*; it is not the momentary wonder of which the Evangelist has just been speaking when he says: 'All that heard it wondered at the things which were spoken unto them by the shepherds': the tense used implies a sustained attitude of mind. This helps us to understand how the phrase comes to be repeated in connection with an incident that occurred twelve years later. All through that time—indeed, we may be sure, all through her life—the mother pondered deeply over the events described in the first two chapters of the Gospel."[†]

The *Magnificat*, which, according to this writer, is far too lyrical and dramatic in character, and too expressive of the traditional Messianic idea to be considered the free composition of St. Luke, throws a new light on the wisdom of Mary. She enters into the thought and hopes of the wise and holy men of Israel with an exultation equal to theirs ("Abraham rejoiced to see my day")—or rather it seems that the thoughts and hopes of the patriarchs and prophets converge and culminate in the *Magnificat*, their ultimate expression. The prophets and patriarchs were, in Israel, what the sages were in heathen lands; they were all that and something much more besides.

As to the guiding and directive side of wisdom, it is almost superfluous to point to the scenes of the Gospel in which Mary stands out with dominating dignity and grace. In the Annunciation Our Lady displays a wondrous self-control; her

---

[†] '"The Virgin-Birth," by Canon William Sanday, which appeared in The Expository Times, an academic journal of theology and biblical studies.

final consent is the result of a kind of treaty with the divine plenipotentiary. At the wedding feast at Cana we see her the embodiment of practical good sense, perfectly mistress of the situation and perfectly mistress of herself. Undismayed by the apparent check to her desires from Our Lord's words, "My hour is not yet come," she calmly gives her order—knowing well that He would do what she wished: "Whatsoever He shall say to you, do ye" (John 2:5). Not to multiply instances, I will only refer to what St. Thomas says about Our Lady's Purification: that she freely wished to observe the legal command for the same reasons as Our Lord Himself, one of which was, "*ut legem approbaret*"— the desire to show approval of the law. Thus, we learn from Our Lady two lessons: reverence for the law and perfect obedience to the law, and both are fruits of the spirit of wisdom.

To the image of Our Lady, drawn from these incidents, our Dominican way of honoring the Queen of heaven adds something further: indeed, from the beginning the Blessed Virgin has always been regarded by us not only as the perfect type, but also as the mistress of wisdom. There is a hint of this in the story of St. Albert the Great. We see him troubled and afraid on account of the vast vista of his knowledge and the devouring curiosity of his mind, insatiable and ever thirsting for more. It is Our Lady, who not only reassures him and urges him to renew the study of wisdom (*sapientiae studio incumbe*), but also shows herself to him in the light of a mistress of learning and custodian of orthodoxy.

Another fact, more simple and familiar, and one which on that very account affords a still stronger proof, is the invocation *Ave Maria* in the margins of those manuscripts of St. Thomas discovered by Uccelli in the last century, inscribed as an appeal to Our Blessed Lady for inspiration.

I am inclined to think that the hesitation which some of our authors seem to have had about supporting the privilege of her Immaculate Conception was a result of so candid and rigid an adherence to principles that it merited the smile of the Saints and of Our Lady herself rather than their frown of surprise. Was not that hesitation the homage of a scrupulous orthodoxy, clinging to the belief that Mary, just as every other child of God, was redeemed by the precious blood of Jesus Christ?

You see, therefore, that the devotion of our Order to the Mother of God is of quite an ideal character. It shows her double function as Mother of the Eternal Wisdom and Spouse of the Holy Ghost prolonged throughout the ages.

There is among all the faithful a deep-rooted conviction that Our Lady has something to do with the justification and salvation of every man, that she has an essential place in the divine economy of grace. This traditional belief gives rise in the present day to a feeling of expectation for a more solemn recognition by the Church of her office as "Mother of Grace." Needless to say, the Dominican school is ready to support and promote this movement. But we are especially and instinctively inclined to contemplate this Maternity of Grace in the Blessed Virgin, in its relation to Light and Wisdom.

Because we owe to her the wonderful account of the Incarnation given to us by St. Luke, we, in a sense, profess to derive from her the very principles of Revelation; consequently, we, in some way, trace back to her testimony the conclusions which Theology draws from revealed principles. In a sense, to her we are indebted for Revelation, considered not only as a grace (because she gave us the Word-made-flesh, which was the supreme Revelation), but also as a divine science. I feel tempted here to quote from Professor Sanday an ingenious inference, which seems almost to prove that the details given by St. Luke could have come only from a woman, that that woman could only have been a confidant of Our Lady's, and that she was, in fact, Joanna, the wife of Chuza. But I wish rather to lay stress upon St. Luke's account as bearing on the dogma of the two natures in Christ, a dogma without which the Gospel is a dead letter, and so conclude that the testimony of Our Blessed Lady is one of the chief foundations of Theology.

Our Lady is not only a mistress of divine science in that fundamental sense, but she is also, if I may use the expression, a *type of Theology*. Our Lord, by uniting in Himself the human and divine, is the Supreme Type of all supernatural life, of the sacramental system, of the constitution and the sanctifying power of the Church, as well as of the interior life of individual souls, so that every moral process in the Church is but a reflected image of His Incarnation. So also Our Blessed Lady, by the wonderful contrast of her prerogatives, by her virginity and her maternity, by her humility and her exaltation above all women, by her holiness and her sorrows, becomes, after Christ, a type of the divine life. In the faith and moral ideas of Christians, the Virgin Mother of God corresponds to God-made-Man. In other words, we do not hesitate to say that, as St. Paul is said to complete the Gospel, so Our Lady completes Christ, reflecting certain delicate rays of moral beauty, shed by the divine glory in the Person of Our Blessed Lord.

Again, being a theological type, Our Lady is the standard, the badge, and touchstone of orthodoxy. To know what is true and reject what is false, it is sometimes enough to turn to the mystery of the Divine Motherhood: heresies cannot stand being confronted with it; they dissolve before that test and it is in this sense, apart from her intercession, that the Church gives her the praise: "*Tu sola interemisti haereses in universo mundo*" ("Thou alone hast destroyed the heresies of all the world"). We can unhesitatingly declare that, in actual practice, our Christian instincts will be blunted, and our Christian virtues will lack grace and dignity and refinement, they will be hard and impoverished, if our devotion to Our Lady is weak or cold.

To conclude: I should like to link up with the title *Seat of Wisdom*, which belongs to Our Lady, a mysterious prerogative proclaimed by innumerable Saints who have excelled in their devotion to her, and which, though not embodied in the textbooks of the schools, is recognized by the faithful in the conversion of thousands of hopeless cases. Our Lady seems to have been entrusted by God with a kind of dispensing power over those terrible and inexorable laws of the moral order, which, after long abuse of grace and much hardness of heart, would, without her help, shut out all hope for the sinner. Often, at a deathbed where the priest has failed to elicit repentance, the sinner has been suddenly converted by the invisible effect of a prayer to Mary. Often, too, those who had lost all faith in and all reverence for Christianity have concealed in their hearts a trace of tender veneration for Our Lady which was the last resource for their salvation. Finally, from certain forms of devotion sanctioned by the Church, we may gather that this mysterious power extends even to Purgatory.

The invocation *Refugium peccatorum* implies, and sums up, all that can be added to these considerations; indeed, it may in a sense be said to be included in the title *Sedes Sapientiae*, because the derogation of a law is preeminently an act of wisdom; for to draw good from evil, to make a saint out of a hopeless sinner, is the triumph of wisdom.

Finally, if wisdom is a sweet savor and a joy, *sapida sapientia*, we must expect the Order, in a great measure, to depend for its joyful spirit of sacrifice, and for its sure instinct for truth, on this heavenly Mistress of wisdom. To be wise—as members of the Order ought to be—is a great thing; but to combine the calm spirit of wisdom with a militant and exultant spirit is a marvel of grace which it would be vain to hope to preserve in the Order but for the ever-inspiring protection of Our Lady, our true and heavenly Minerva! Pray that the Order be more and more the fortress of truth, that each of us be more truly a knight of the Mother of Wisdom, and, after the battle of life, we may die, protected by her shield, retiring from the battlefield to the strains of the *Salve Regina*!

XVI

A Lesson from the Deathbed and Tomb of St. Dominic

When the Church pays honor to the remains of the Saints; when, for example, she translates them with pomp and ceremony, she wishes not only to invite us to venerate their relics, but also to draw a lesson from their memory. Even when, for mere social or natural reasons, we gather round an illustrious tomb, there is not just homage to be paid, but also a lesson to be learnt. On a tombstone we read at a glance the whole story of a life, its chief moral features and its meaning. In this we find one of the many reasons that justify the veneration of relics. Now at the first translation of the body of St. Dominic, so touchingly described by Blessed Jordan, there took place, as you know, a wonderful manifestation of the merits of our holy Father's life. The miraculous perfume which clung to the hands of Blessed Jordan was a lesson as well as a testimony. Lesson and testimony—both teach and attest his admirable purity.

But to seize the full meaning of that lesson we must connect that heavenly testimony with the last recommendations of St. Dominic on his deathbed.

Just as St. Francis, when dying, desired to be laid naked on the ashes, so St. Dominic on his deathbed, by an act of sublime simplicity, strips his soul before our eyes. It is sad to see modern historians, blind to the beauty of that scene, toning down its most striking features. Père Lacordaire is perhaps among the few who have gauged its true significance. St. Dominic, to lay stress on the counsel he gives to his children, begins by revealing to them the jealous esteem in which he has always held the virtue of purity, and owns that he has received the grace of perfect virginity of body and soul. Then, unexpectedly, he adds that nevertheless he was no stranger to the charm of youth in woman. I do not think that it was to avert a remote temptation to vainglory that such an admission came from his lips, and still less was it remorse for the slightest formal sin against purity. St. Dominic had reached that degree of humility which does not tremble under divine favors. The hint of self-reproach, coming after the public avowal of his special graces, could have but one meaning. It is only the test of his exquisite sense of the spiritual detachment from things human, required of a soul about to draw near to the possession of God. At the moment of entering into the eternal espousals, the instinct of purity in St. Dominic becomes transfigured; he begins by speaking of purity in the ordinary sense of the word, and then rises to that absolute simplicity of soul which crowns the preparation of the elect.

Simplicity is indeed the word to use here, for simplicity shines out in St. Dominic's utter candor and is the proof of his entire detachment. So, from his deathbed to his tomb, we follow the whole scale of purity; first, purity as a special virtue and as the matter of the religious vow; secondly, purity as a higher degree of spiritual detachment and as a general virtue; purity almost identified with the angelic life in heaven, and glorified by the miraculous fragrance. Let us dwell on the great lesson these thoughts inculcate.

Why do the saints of the Middle Ages speak so openly, and sometimes so realistically, of purity, while a Doctor of the Church, living in the time of the Renaissance, classes purity among the virtues of which one should not speak? Was it a result of the rude simplicity of those ages? Refined though we may be, we have no right to think so. Apart from all the other reasons, it was especially fitting that our Order, the Order of truth, should give a forcible illustration of those words of Our Lord: "Blessed are the pure in heart, for they shall see God." The austerities of our Order are inspired chiefly by the motive of protecting its purity. You know how St. Thomas, asserting the traditional teaching of the Church, links together purity and the light of the mind. Besides, the men of the Middle Ages did not think of purity in any merely limited and rudimentary sense. It is rather by the men of our own day that the vow of chastity is looked on as a mere negative act of renunciation: to our first fathers it was a glorious consecration. In the form of our profession the vow of chastity is not explicitly mentioned, but, so to say, embodied in the homage of our whole life by the vow of obedience. The purity to which we are vowed does not merely draw us from the ranks of animality, but places us in God's reserve; just as the most lovely blossoms are snatched from the law of reproduction to become things of beauty.

St. Thomas Aquinas takes us a step further in his doctrine of purity. When drawing from the Epistle to the Galatians his teaching upon the fruits of the Holy Ghost, he gives chastity its place among them. A fruit is an ultimate perfection, a final and peaceful delight, the enjoyment of what is good and the quelling of what is evil: "*aliquid ultimum—fruitionem bonorum et seda-tionem malorum, quod videtur ad rationem fructus pertinere*" (see *Summa Theologiae*, I–II.70, a. 3).

Such perfection and such delight evidently result, in the first place, because the vow and the virtue have become easy and almost instinctive; they imply that we are acclimatized to the spiritual life which leads to that realm where the friends of God are as the Angels in heaven—they neither marry nor are given in marriage. We belong to God, and we feel the joy of belonging to Him. The uplifting to a higher life necessarily has a joy of its own.

The taste of this spiritual fruit should be perceived to some extent by all Christians who practice, according to their state, this holy virtue; as St. Paul says to all: "I have espoused you to one husband, that I may present you as a chaste virgin to Christ." It is the grace of baptism that produces such fruits. Yet, since the religious life is the perfection of the Christian life, the fruit of purity should have a finer flavor for us. We may recall here the teaching of St. Thomas, that religious profession is a second Baptism washing away all past sin through the charity with which it is embraced. Consequently we should deem ourselves young and renewed, as if our lives had begun afresh on the day we made profession. The sense of belonging to God admits thenceforth of no shadow of doubt. Nor is there now any possibility of withdrawal. We definitely belong to a new kingdom. We have a right to a special intimacy with God. If we rarely experience this privilege and joy, there is ground to fear that we have not understood the real nature of our dedication.

If, as sometimes happens, an unfortunate religious turns back in search of earthly joys and falls so low as to desert the paradise of Dominican life, it is because little by little he has lost the taste for the fruits of the divine Spirit. We need to awaken in ourselves the glad consciousness of what we are and of our relation to God; this should be our defense in all our trials and perils.

The lesson of purity goes further still; it can be considered as a general virtue in the sense of the words of St. Thomas: *In quadam spirituali conjunctione mentis ad res aliquas consistit quaedam delectatio, circa quam est quaedam spiritualis castitas, metaphorice dicta*—"There are many things with which mental contact is a source of joy, about which, metaphorically speaking, there is a kind of spiritual chastity" (*Summa Theologiae*, II–II.151, a. 2). That general virtue which represents in our spiritual lives the sense of honor. *Potius mori quam foedari*. We are all aware of the importance in our social relations of a high sense of honor; its object is not always adequate to that of Christian morality, and yet, within the sphere in which it acts, it gives to the natural character a strength and delicacy that, indeed, sad to say, is not always conspicuous in some Christians. The sense of honor is fidelity transformed into an invincible passion and jealousy. It presupposes, therefore, in one way or another, a great love. In effect St. Thomas adds that purity, as a general virtue, comes from divine charity: "*principaliter ratio hujus castitatis consistit in charitate*" (see *Summa Theologiae*, II–II.151, a. 2). It is solely the love of God that can inspire the desire to refrain from lawful and innocent pleasures. Here purity is not only the defense of our vocation, not only the happiness of belonging to God, but also the most intense satisfaction of the desires of the soul. It becomes a latent and exquisite heroism which, not content with the sacrifice implied in the slaying of concupiscence, seeks ever to accomplish the holocaust of nature on the altar of charity. Such thoughts give meaning to St. Dominic's deathbed avowal. The purity which wins, even after death, the heavenly approval of that miraculous fragrance, is purity carried to this high degree of heroic holiness.

Few have perceived or expressed the lesson of purity left to us by St. Dominic in the same way as St. Catherine of Siena. In her Dialogue she points out that purity is an indispensable condition for carrying out the purpose of the Order. "Since impure living obscures the eye of the intellect, and not only the eye of the intellect, but also of the body, he does not wish them to obscure their physical light, with which they may more perfectly obtain the light of science; wherefore he imposed on them the third vow of continence, and wishes that all should observe it with true and perfect obedience." What strength in that woman's hand which traces both the negative and prepa-ratory character of purity and its illuminative power! How the Dominican note rings through it! From St. Dominic himself on his deathbed we have another promise of a special blessing on our perseverance in the virtue of purity: "The spotlessness of your lives will ensure you great triumphs among men." His very tomb was the first pledge of this promise. The relics of him who was detached from all the things of earth and whose purity had made him a light and a flame, were enshrined in a sepulcher of which the perfection and beauty are a triumph of the art of man. The greatest masters, representatives of the best periods of Italian sculpture, produced by the originality and the power of their execution a monument comparable to the ancient master-pieces. Michelangelo brought the offering of his genius, as if the mighty sadness of his soul sought rest on that tomb. Every scene and figure radiates intellectual vigor, and the whole is a triumph of the idea of wisdom, harmony, and life. Here, on the tomb of this purest of men, is solved the problem of the union of human art with its supernatural expression. As you kneel at that tomb you feel in your soul the sweet odor of the virginal virtues of St. Dominic, and when you rise up you are comforted and spurred to work valiantly.

Ask our Father St. Dominic to obtain for us that we may never forget the lesson he taught us in his last words. Implore him to help us to carry them out in our lives, with the perfection symbolized by the sweet fragrance commemorated in this Feast of his Translation.

O *lumen Ecclesiae, doctor veritatis, rosa patientiae, ebur castitatis, aquam sapientiae propinasti gratis: praedicator gratiae, nos junge beatis.*

O light of the Church, teacher of Truth, rose of patience, ivory of chastity. You freely poured forth the waters of wisdom. Preacher of grace, unite us with the blessed.

XVII

Dominican Loyalty to the Church

It is interesting to study St. Dominic's relations with the Holy See, and to note the number of papal documents issued in his favor. The Church looks with real benevolence towards the newly-founded Order, and St. Dominic is firm and insistent in submitting the Order absolutely to the control and authority of the Sovereign Pontiff. The year 1219 is especially rich in letters of recommendation from Pope Honorius III to the Bishops and Prelates, not of Spain and France only but of the universal Church. In his personal struggles with the University and Chapter of Paris, St. Dominic would seem to have almost succeeded in winning over the Pope to his side. We must also mention a Bull of December 12, of the same year, which may be called our *Charter of Indulgence*. This Bull allowed the labors and penitential works of the Order to be accounted to all its members in satisfaction for their sins. Often afterwards the Holy See expresses in a special manner its gratitude towards the benefactors of the Order. The Church, as it were, makes compensation for her first resistance to St. Dominic's enterprise; it was also a promising sign foreshadowing the future adoption of the Order by Gregory IX as a universal instrument of the Roman Church. In passing, it may be said that we do not yet know in detail all that Gregory IX did for us; I mean, as regards his influence on our interior organization. May I also add that the Order, from its very origin, had a clear and definite consciousness of its being organically united with the Holy See? This is why it preserved its unity and its immunity from the aberrations of individual mysticism. The preservation of its unity should be noted as no small reward for its loyalty.

To maintain this precious tradition our first duty is to see in the Church a personal and intelligent messenger of Divine Truth—and then joyfully submit to her authority, and love her voice as that of a mother.

Among those—an ever-increasing number—who admit the collective and ecclesiastical character of Christianity, there are comparatively few who adequately understand the nature and personality of the Church. Every social body is morally a person—a *persona moralis*; I mean that, of its very nature, a corporate body, like a person, must determine for itself certain notions of goodness, truth, and justice, which by its Constitution are enforced on all, without appeal, as the society's essential principles of social life. Now whatever share individuals may take in the development and applications of those principles in ordinary associations of men, whatever may be the impulse of nature itself in forming such societies, the fact remains that the form and measure of their acceptance are nothing more than the result of the general collective tendency of the race and of the necessities and conventions of social life. In the end personality vanishes and only convention survives: expedients and makeshifts displace rules, and no laws are regarded as absolute or final. Even when authority is absolute and the human group becomes more conscious of its tradition and genius, it always remains an artificial society and what is technically termed a *moral* body.

Now this does not apply with regard to the Church. On the contrary, with the Church the constructive process is, neither in its beginning nor in its conclusion, a matter of convention or merely collective arrangement. Her Constitution comes from one Thought and one Will, from One Divine Person. Human traditions and merely national interests have no part in upholding her principles, since she derives her principles from the Absolute Truth, and includes all races within her catholicity. The force of her decisions and her laws is not due to, or limited by, the necessity of avoiding endless appeals, but by the necessities of the Eternal Reason and the Eternal Law.

All this does not exclude the contributions of the children of the Church to the elucidation of the great message she delivers to the world, nor does it exclude the deliberations of Councils, nor the disputes between various theological schools. But the results of private research add nothing to the substance of the message. They are only preliminaries to the Canons of Councils and to the pontifical definitions which do but present in a clearer light one or another of the aspects of Revelation. All these voices, of theologians and private doctors, which are raised from various points of the compass, are but notes of a chorus that accompanies one leading voice. Or rather, those forms of expression, until sanctioned and incorporated by the Church, may truly be said to be in themselves of no importance in their bearing on Revelation. They are not unlike *materia prima*, which does not exist in itself, is inconceivable without form, and is *fere nihil*—next door to nothing.

So truly is the Church a *Person*, that her infallible voice is the voice of one infallible man. The Church is not only a Person, but, as I have said, an intelligent one. She is not a mere instrument of the Living Voice that speaks through her. The Spirit, through whose divine assistance she acts, confers on her all the marks of an intelligent Personality; perfect clearness of vision, perfect consciousness of her rights and duties, directive and motive power, freedom and vigor, power to resist, defend, and attack. Just as, in the inspired writers, the Holy Ghost suppresses no element of their personality, so in the Church He unites the divine and human in a unity which recalls the unity of Christ. Moreover, He merges the elements of the Church's life, scattered through the ages, into a wonderful continuity, stamped with unfailing self-recollection, and with unerring logic. Routine and convention cannot account for this!

The personal and intelligent character of the Church cannot be ignored without lowering revelation to the level of a pure fiction, at the mercy of every wind that blows, and successively embodying in itself the childish errors or the subtle speculations of the different stages of human history. Without going so far, certain Catholics tend to see in the Church a mere passive organ, to which private learning and scientific criticism furnish the matter of an unconscious elaboration. Others go so far as to deny to the Church all insight into spiritual reality through rational ideas, and they see in her teaching and doctrinal decisions nothing more than practical commands without any reference to objective and divine Truth. This is no place for controversy, but the motive which originated such incredible statements can easily be discerned: it is the wish to cover, and consecrate in the name of the Church, all the unbridled license of a criticism hostile to theological tradition. Such an attempt is an insult not only to the Church but also to the Divine Intelligence which guides her, and which in such a case would, when speaking through the Church, speak in order to say nothing.[1]

---

†   This was written and delivered on the very eve of the appearance of Pope St. Pius X's Encyclical Letter Pascendi Dominici Gregis (On the Doctrine of the Modernists).

If there are difficulties regarding obedience to the Church—a possibility I am far from denying—let us see in what they consist, and how to overcome them.

First, we often forget the true nature of supernatural obedience. To obey is to conform our will to the will of God, but it is in very exceptional cases that the Divine Will intimates its decisions to a man without any intermediary. The Divine Will is universal; attentive as it is to individual interests, it works for the general good in and through the particular good. It does not overstep the action of secondary causes; on the contrary, it directs all their concentric spheres towards an end which contains both the individual and the general good. The Divine Will is supernatural: it tends to results which, though they do not always contradict, yet always transcend the natural good of creatures.

From these two principles it follows, first, that in the human intermediaries of the Divine Will we have not to consider their own personal perfection, but only what they command; second, in the results of supernatural obedience we have not to consider their immediate value, but only the certainty that we cannot gauge their real worth. How often, on the contrary, not knowing our place in the divine economy, do we presumptuously desire the direct intervention of God, and wish to obey only on condition that we see the immediate results of God's Will! We must remember that the Divine Will, acting through a vast assembly of causes, does not change their limited and imperfect nature. God puts up with the deficiencies of His agents with more patience than we do, and He maintains them in united action.

Consequently, obedience reaches God through this same assembly of causes, and we must expect it to meet on its way imperfections, shocks, and delays; and obedience itself misses the standard of the real worth of its results, except that it knows them to be supernatural. The life of the Church is a living object

lesson and an illustration of this theory of obedience. The Divine
Authority, which speaks through the Church, adapts itself to the
conditions of time and place. It calls its agents and intermediaries from every race and country, from every class of men. It
sometimes seems that the Church does not always lead the course
of history, but often follows it. Thus the Church, in her work of
transmitting the Divine Commands, acts in varying and inter-
mittent ways; now spontaneously and unexpectedly; now slowly,
constrained by heresy; now as the universal and dogmatic teacher
of men; now by deductive and directive methods; now by definitions of faith; now by the decrees of Congregations; now yielding
somewhat to the tenets of some particular school of theology;
now, apparently, giving much credit to some historical system,
either overly critical or overly credulous. Finally, the Divine Will
shows, by the spoliations and persecutions which it permits the
Church to go through, that in working for supernatural results it
does not need temporal riches and earthly glory, that it does not
depend upon great buildings, or set store by artistic treasure even
for the shrines of the Saints, that it does not trust in prosperous
and wealthy enterprises even for the sake of apostolic work.

Obedient Christians will not be scandalized by these different
modes of action. They will remember that obedience is due not
to the considerations alleged in support of the social order but to
the all-comprehending Reason, which never fails in the long run
to obtain the most desirable result for all. It never fails to reward
adequately those who render to it an adequate obedience.

A more common difficulty comes from the lack of filial
dispositions on the part of Christians. Supernatural obedience
implies nobility and tenderness; otherwise, it is servile. He who
is truly obedient has the right to discern the different forms
and measures through which the Divine Will manifests itself to
him; but he makes allowance for the circumstances; he thinks

of possible motives unknown to him; he has sufficient tact not to forestall the censures of History. Above all, he has too great a devotion to the Church not to correct, in his heart, by the generosity of his acceptance, the imperfect orders given to him. True obedience looks clearly and steadily at the authority of the superior and the command he gives. Simple obedience should be given without any thought of private and personal advantage or of the results that may follow. Such obedience, even to the unwise command of an imperfect superior, achieves more than obedience given in a more human spirit to an order which may commend itself by all the motives of sound sense and human prudence that may seem to have inspired it.

The imperfectly obedient man takes a mischievous pleasure in the circumstances that tell unfavorably against the Church in the exercise of her authority; he carefully dissects the considerations on which the Church's precepts are based; he barters his docility; above all, he wishes and hopes that the judgments of the Church will ere long be reversed. No authority on earth could carry out its mission if it depended on such obedience. It is not obedience of this kind that a true Dominican should offer to the Church.

By way of conclusion let me add just two remarks: nobility and tenderness will triumph not only over the difficulties of obedience but also over the imperfections of the commands of authority. Experience proves that lack of loyalty, besides being a fault, is a fruitful source of misunderstanding. A bad spirit shows want of tact; it leads to an awkward manner of approach in applying to authority; it inevitably means indiscretion, restlessness, not to speak of petty deceits and the miserable methods of "diplomacy"; in a word it spells failure. We have the superiors we deserve. He who is truly obedient will be able, when occasion requires, like St. Paul, to remonstrate openly with his superiors; but he will leave them no room for doubt, either as to his motives and goodwill or as to his unfailing loyalty.

We must not only love the Church as a Mother but also idealize her, and drive from us every thought of suspicion and diffidence. Let us remember St. Paul proclaiming the Church *"without spot or wrinkle, or any such thing,"* and, after him, St. Augustine saying that the Church is a virgin, and that the practice of purity in the Church is only an imitation of the virginity of her Faith.

A doctrinal Order, such as ours, is specially bound to the authority of the Church, since she expects much from us, and to her we owe much, since we share so closely the responsibility of delivering her divine message.

Let us not forget the recognition of our great vocation as Champions of the Faith, lovingly voiced by Pope Leo XIII almost every year of his glorious pontificate. What a wonderful chance that was for the revival of our Order! What an opportunity lost! Is it lost forever? We hope not.

Our vocation as Champions of the Faith impels us to strive, by our generous and loyal devotion to the Church, to make our Order a bulwark of Christendom.

XVIII

Conclusion

Thus shalt thou say to the house of Jacob and tell the children of Israel: you have seen what I have done to the Egyptians, how I have carried you upon the wings of eagles and have taken you to myself (Exodus 19:3–4).

The more faithful we are to our ideal and the further it recedes from us, the deeper is the sense of our own utter incapacity to realize it in ourselves. In the first place, its realization seems to demand a triple personality to enable us to live up to its three-fold character; and, in the second, the spirit of the day, tending as it does to division and specialization, would seem to lead us to develop and absorb ourselves in one or other of the elements of our life to the detriment of the others. This feeling may, at times, expose us to the temptation to discouragement or perplexity.

During the course of this exposition of principles I have laid such stress on each of these elements and brought each in turn into such a strong light that you may have lost the sense of their unity, and you may ask yourselves how they are to be fused into one. Shall I tell you? By fidelity of heart to each and all. In practice we may, under special circumstances, be obliged to devote ourselves almost exclusively to one or other of the threefold duties of our life; but if we preserve in our hearts an unflinching fidelity to the Dominican ideal it is impossible for us not to succeed in stamping our particular work with the integral spirit of our vocation. I beg you therefore to hold passionately to the true conception of our Dominican life and to hold it in all its beauty and integrity.

Our vocation is not just to one accidental variety of the religious life: it is a new entity, a new type, a new species, which results from the substantial transformation of its component parts into one. Precisely therein lies the originality of the work of St. Dominic. Consequently there is no Dominican substance where either of these elements is lacking.

Even if to unite them in practice were just a dream it would be a dream so beautiful as to be worth living for.

Just as the eaglet is confronted with the sun to test its fitness to live, so you are confronted with this great ideal to test the reality of your vocation. I firmly believe that we shall have to give a still more strict account of our fidelity to this theoretical ideal than we shall of the practical accomplishment of any of its parts. Love for the integrity of our ideal will cover a multitude of sins.

So you see no discouragement is admissible. There is not one among us who has not at some moment of his life possessed in himself the fullness of the Dominican character. During the years of our religious training the idea of the Order took possession of us; and, as it is written that the kingdom of God is within, so we might say that the Order was, at one time, embodied in us. The freedom which comes from perfect detachment, the joy of daily contact with things divine, ardent enthusiasm for the study of Truth were all stamped on us, and held out to us a great promise. But a critical moment comes, when we have to pass from this perfect life to one more individual and more predominantly active; and then comes the danger of dismemberment and the disintegration of our forces.

Then, we have neither time nor love for the interior life; we lose first the taste, and then little by little even the capacity for study. I know no Order in which this transition is so dangerous as in ours. Yet the fact remains that we have once been raised to a full comprehension of the ideal of the Order, and consequently lifted to a higher degree of spiritual personality. There is none of us who does not owe to the Order more than he could ever, or can ever, gain outside it; even those who desert the Order continue to owe everything to it.

"I have carried you upon the wings of eagles."

Let us press forward to develop within ourselves the perfect image of a Dominican, otherwise the world itself will rob us of our glory, as has happened more than once before. During the violent periods of religious upheavals we are deprived of our houses and dispersed; but this is not the hardest part of the chastisement that falls upon us. When calm settles on the land, then begins the true spoliation, then the world usurps our functions and transposes them to secular uses. To illustrate this assertion look at the way Anglicanism has now usurped the rites of Catholicism, and even the very name which once it loathed. Glorious as are the Universities of this country, we cannot but see in them an instance of the transfer into an almost purely human sphere of the ancient conception of the studious life; a life consecrated by the Church and cherished by our Order. One cannot enter the peaceful cloisters of Oxford without feeling this, and without sadness at our loss. Our ideal, which with stress and strain we evoke from the past, and feel powerless to reconstitute in its full splendor, it is there, there, in cloisters, chapels, libraries, halls, and gardens, now in the hands of those to whom our true ideal is almost unknown, even while they claim to embody it.

However, let us never doubt the everlasting power of that Science which it falls to our lot to draw from revealed truths, to develop through metaphysical principles, and to conciliate with all branches of human knowledge. Let not the torch pass from our hands to those of others. What a mournful pity it would be were we, through discouragement, to abdicate our doctrinal prerogatives and to be disloyal to the Absolute Truth, just at the time when there are so many signs of a return to the science of the absolute! You know that nowadays men eminent in science openly avow that physical science—I mean pure physics rather than astronomy or geology—is not explanatory, but representative of reality. Mathematical values in physical science are said to be like the lines of a sketch, each stroke of which, if taken alone, gives no true impression of Nature, but altogether they approximate to likeness. Only some years ago there was a tendency to make of the mechanical and mathematical interpretation of nature an equation of reality: now they say that science, as it progresses, tends to reality, but tends after the manner of a work of art. Such a position is as far removed from scientific mechanism as from skepticism. Now, they admit that physics and metaphysics proceed equally from human common sense, and, though never identified, represent, each in its own way, an aspect of reality. They even go so far as to say that science is the poetry of a world grown old. We need not fear the attacks of criticism on our theological principles any more than we do those of natural science. Criticism, in its turn, is beginning to show that it is vitiated by subjectivism. It condenses detailed observations in general statements which are, at times, nothing more than words—or at any rate have little relation to the facts they sum up. When we are told that there is a *"Johannine Question,"* when we hear of the *"Eschatology"* of the Gospels, of the *sporadic* character of certain teachings of Our Lord in the sacred text, such headings sound far more imposing and significant than would the simple names formerly given to the difficulties which may be found in this or that inspired book. Even when they are other than verbal generalizations, even when their contents are more real than mere impressions, they must not arrogate only to themselves reality and refuse it to metaphysical and philosophical axioms and principles.

Moreover, our scientific tradition is wide enough to embrace all the well-justified conclusions of natural science, just as it is too high to be reached by science falsely so called. Those who maintain that the thirteenth century arrested the scientific movement inaugurated in the eleventh by Silvester II, strangely forget the names of St. Albert the Great and Roger Bacon.

Our scientific traditions are in no way opposed to research or to experimental observation, but our investigation of nature and natural phenomena is carried out mainly in the light of their highest causes. The very broadness of our principles is a pledge of the respect we pay to Science and the appeal we make to a harmony of all spheres of study into a higher synthesis.

"I have carried you upon the wings of eagles."

Not only are our learned men as eagles, but still more our Saints. Let not the world surpass us in appreciation and admiration of them. It is humiliating to see merely secular artists and writers revealing to the sons of the Saints the glory of their fathers. Even as a return to scholastic doctrines seems probable, so also ere long the world will make the *discovery* of our Saints.

For my part I have no wish to see our Saints become the hobby of fashionable writers and worldly readers. We ought to have more pride than to let the world explore and exploit our treasures, reveal to us their beauty, and share with us their precious worth. A serious study of our Saints, a more complete comprehension of their spirit and action, a more living insight into their historic environment, all these are indeed needed; but ours the right and the duty to carry out the task. We ought to reproduce in ourselves their character, and become their living images in the eyes of the people.

In close union with fidelity to the spirit of our Saints is fidelity to the ascetical and mystical traditions of our Order. Here in particular there is a huge task to be undertaken, as the world is starving for the strong food of the soul. Nowadays practical faith, interior life, and prayer lack both their true objects and their sure foundation. I sum up in one sentence all that is to be done, and the reason of its necessity: Spirituality attained through exposition of principles is more needed and far more efficacious than spirituality derived from empiric rules and devotional impulses.

Think well of this. Remember that it is your duty to raise yourselves and the souls committed to your care to the heights where supernatural life springs fresh and pure from Divine Truth. "I have carried you upon the wings of eagles." "I have taken you to Myself." It is said that Our Lord went up alone on to a mountain to pray, and spent the night in prayer. It is said again that He, at times, took His disciples with Him on to the mountain; but, in truth, His prayer was always solitary. His Blessed Soul was always on the mountain of the Hypostatic Union. Even when He teaches His disciples to pray, and condescends to express for them their own needs, even then the prayer He teaches them— the Lord's Prayer—seems to be the echo of His own sublime converse with His Father. The first part of that prayer remains mysterious and inexhaustible, like the prayer of the Divine Solitary. It is one of the wonderful aspects of the Gospel that it shows us Our Lord as the friend of the poor, the ignorant, and the sinner, and, at the same time, far removed from the mass of mankind, and far above popularity. We, being called to know and contemplate the Divine Truth, are bound to share to some degree the inner life of the Soul of the Incarnate Word. We have been taken to Himself, and "Nothing shall separate us from the Truth and Charity of Christ."

This call is a difficult ascent which implies that, as we mount upwards, we must cast from us many things—the last remnants of attachment to all that is earthly or human. It implies that even our faith in Our Lord and our devotion to Him have, in a sense, to be purified more and more. As I have already said, our Ideal recedes from us, so also Our Lord recedes from us, in the measure that we draw near to Him. "Flee away, my Beloved," cries the Spouse in the Canticle; and St. Thomas, on his death-bed, thus expresses the truth contained in those words:

> *Flee away*, that is, having accomplished the mystery of Thine Incarnation and Passion, return to Heaven, that from henceforth I may think of Thee as the God who is above all. Then shalt Thou hear my voice, because there will I preach Thee with freedom to the whole world. This is indeed what Our Lord intends when He says: "Verily I say to you, it is expedient for you that I go away." For it was expedient for the Apostles, and for the Church, that Christ should go away, that is, should withdraw His visible Presence, because, when present in the Body, they could not love Him in a purely spiritual way. "*Non poterant eum spiritualiter amare.*"

But after He had ascended to Heaven, the Church began to love Him in a purely spiritual way, to think of Him as God, and to preach Him as God. This is what the Apostle means when he says: "If we have known Christ according to the flesh, but now we know Him so no longer." Therefore, O my Beloved, if Thou willest that I preach Thee thus, flee away, withdraw Thyself to Heaven; and Thou, who through Thy Humanity became comprehensible, be Thou incomprehensible through Thy Divinity: "*recede ad caelestia, et qui fuisti comprehensibilis per humanitatem, efficere incomprehensibilis per divinitatem.*" (Commentary of St. Thomas Aquinas in *Cantica Canticorum* when he was dying.)

You see to what heights fidelity to the Absolute lifts us. It leads us to the perfection of those virtues which have God for their direct object: it makes us walk in pure Faith; it gives our Hope fresh ardor, and makes us love for His own sake the Supreme Good. Thus is our dedication to God accomplished. "I have taken you to Me."

Benedicat manum scribentis
Lingua devote legentis.[†]

---

†   "May the tongue of one speaking devoutly bless the hand of the one writing."

CLUNY MEDIA

Designed by Fiona Cecile Clarke, the CLUNY MEDIA *logo*
depicts a monk at work in the scriptorium,
with a cat sitting at his feet.

The monk represents our mission to emulate
the invaluable contributions of the monks
of Cluny in preserving the libraries of the West,
our strivings to know and love the truth.

The cat at the monk's feet is Pangur Bán, from the
eponymous Irish poem of the 9th century.
The anonymous poet compares his scholarly
pursuit of truth with the cat's happy hunting of mice.
The depiction of Pangur Bán is an homage to the work
of the monks of Irish monasteries and a sign
of the joy we at Cluny take in our trade.

"Messe ocus Pangur Bán,
cechtar nathar fria saindan:
bíth a menmasam fri seilgg,
mu memna céin im saincheirdd."

Made in the USA
Middletown, DE
22 August 2021